Atheism Today
A Christian Response

Bernard Tyrrell, S.J.

and

John Navone, S.J.

IP

ITHACA PRESS

NEW YORK

Atheism Today
A Christian Response

This book uses the Revised Standard Version of the Bible.

Ithaca Press
3 Kimberly Drive, Suite B
Dryden, New York 13053 USA
www.IthacaPress.com

Cover Design   Gary Hoffman
Book Design   Gary Hoffman

Manufactured in the United States of America

9 8 7 6 5 4 3 2 1

Library of Congress Cataloging-in-Data Available

First Edition

Printed in the United States of America

ISBN   978-0-9839121-5-6

www.AtheismTodayAChristianResponse.com
www.BernardTyrrellSJ.com
www.JohnNavoneSJ.com

Dedication

To my dear friends and major benefactors
Linda and Michael Mewhinney
And with loving mention of
Fred Crowell, and Thomas Carroll.

Bernard Tyrrell, S. J.

To my friend Thomas Aquinas Maier, Chair of the Hospitality
Department of DePaul University, Chicago.
And with loving mention my sisters Helen Gleason and
Catherine Mullally, and my brothers Joseph, James, and George.

John Navone, S. J.

Acknowledgements

The authors acknowledge their profound gratitude for the expert advice and gracious assistance of Sarah DeSimone that proved indispensable for shaping the finished product that is our book.

We also express our deep appreciation for the technical assistance and boundless patience of Michael Rorholm, the business manager of our Jesuit House community at Gonzaga University.

Table of Contents

Preface

Atheism Today: A Christian Response is a must read for anyone interested in and concerned about the attacks that the so-called New Atheism of Richard Dawkins, Christopher Hitchens, Sam Harris, Daniel Dennett and others have made against Christianity and the other monotheistic religions. Their militant rhetoric receives widespread attention in our culture and spreads like wild-fire through the constant coverage provided by the media. The two authors, Bernard Tyrrell and John Navone, offer the reader an insightful approach toward understanding the context of contemporary atheism as well as providing the Christian believer-thinker with critical answers to their views and attacks. The authors' aim is not to engage contemporary atheists in stringent, strident attacks in the same manner that Christians were addressed. Instead, the thoughts of these two well-respected Jesuit-scholars and prolific writers, Bernard Tyrrell and John Navone, empower the educated Christian with insights and responses.

Without doubt the structure of this book contributes to its uniqueness and originality. The authors have chosen to address some thirty-eight areas that lie at the heart of the attacks made by contemporary atheists. Tyrrell and Navone have chosen to respond to these attacks in concise and erudite ways that give Christian readers insight into their own Christian thought, traditions, and beliefs in a much deeper and authentic way. What I found so fascinating was the gift of seeing two different authors approaching a topic of concern from two distinct perspectives. Each offers an insight that

Bernard Tyrrell, S. J.   John Navone, S. J.

connects with the other while at the same time contributing something unique to the discussion.

Let me offer one gem I selected from the range of areas of discussion they covered. This gem provides a beautiful illustration of how the thought of these authors dovetails and contributes to a deeper insight into the area of their reflections. In chapter one, "Initial Reflections," Tyrrell clearly identifies the problem with contemporary atheists. He shows that they reject "any data that they cannot empirically test with their limited methods of verification." Using the thought of the philosopher-theologian Bernard Lonergan, Tyrrell shows where their fallacy lies. God is not some object to be analyzed, but rather God is the very foundation of and explanation for what exists. It is not God who needs to be explained, but existence itself. In a similar vein, John Navone provides his "Initial Reflections." He points to how these New Atheists call Christians and all believers "delusional, as being out of touch with what is real." However, Navone turns the argument on them by showing that they are the ones who are out of touch with the very experience of billions of human beings throughout history whose lives have been based on "the transcendent reality that grounds their existence." Navone provides a very insightful context for understanding contemporary atheism by reminding the reader that atheism is a relatively new phenomenon in human history. In fact, in the long line of human history, atheism is the anomaly, not religious belief.

For those seeking responses to the attacks that contemporary atheism has made on Christian believers this in an indispensable book. No thoughtful Christian can afford to ignore the dialogue provided by these two extremely insightful and well-respected scholars who draw upon the wealth of their experience, reflections, and knowledge.

Father Patrick J Hartin
Professor of Religious Studies
Gonzaga University
Spokane, WA

Introduction

Why this book when there are so many books dealing roughly with similar issues? This book is unique in its brevity and format and in the distinct, but complementary intellectual backgrounds of its authors. Our book offers an example of two authors in dialogue. By introducing a second voice, our dialogue becomes a conversation through which my coauthor, John Navone, in his thoughtful responses jump-starts one's own reflections. His voice highlights the two-way process of any reading in which the reader has a right to be different. It is more a difference of emphasis, perspective, and tone. Our collaborative approach debunks the idea that problems are solved or questions answered in isolation. It is written in generally 1,000 to 1,600 words per chapter. We agreed that one of us would write an initial critique of some significant objection to the existence of God/religion by a contemporary atheist or several atheists and the other would offer a reflection on some issue relevant to the chapter topic. Diverse views are an antidote to blinkered thinking.

In terms of our backgrounds my doctoral degree is in philosophy and Navone's doctoral degree is in theology. We are both Jesuits and we have similar Master's degrees or their equivalents in both philosophy and theology. John Navone taught at the Gregorian University in Rome for forty years and is a remarkably prolific author of some twenty-two books and countless articles. I am in my thirty-ninth year of teaching at Gonzaga University and am chiefly known for my books on Christotherapy and Bernard Lonergan. We are both influenced by a variety of philosophers and theologians, but the philosophy and theology of Thomas Aquinas and Bernard Lonergan have heavily influenced both of us. I should mention that I had the blessing of studying under both Bernard Lonergan and Karl Rahner. The two were born in 1904 and died in 1984. Rahner deeply influenced me also. Navone and I differ in that philosophy within a theological framework is my basic métier, whereas theology within a biblical framework is Navone's basic métier. Of course, both of us frequently crossover into one another's territory because of our common educational backgrounds and interests.

This book is intended for the educated reader, not just for specialists. Our aim here is to offer critical responses to contemporary atheists in a brief, concise, and hopefully compelling fashion. An ever growing number of contemporary atheists are aggressively militant in their attacks on the existence of a transcendent divine principle or God and specifically on the God of the monotheist religions, with a special laser-like focus on Christianity and its Judaic forbearers. They also criticize Islam. The names most frequently mentioned are bestselling authors Richard Dawkins, Christopher Hitchens, Sam Harris, and Daniel Dennett, but of late there are many more waiting in the wings for similar recognition and we are often offering a critique of them too. The most recent widely publicized achievement of the latter is the establishment of an International Blasphemy Day to be held each year on September 30.

Most importantly, the book is not just about atheism and its criticisms, but it also strives to shed light on the inexhaustible riches of the Good News of Jesus Christ in which the Father is revealed through the gift of the Holy Spirit. The positive aspects of this book result from our studies of the theologians mentioned above. Rahner and Lonergan both named God as Mystery. They were both very ecumenical in their writings and each in his own way endeavored to show that a pre-conceptual faith, given by the Holy Spirit, is at work in all human beings of good will. We must mention, however, that we do use apologetics or strong defenses of our faith in dealing with the militant atheists so active today. Paul in Ephesians tells us to put on the armor that God gives us, to fight for the Word of God and to let faith be like a shield and our sword be the message of God, which comes from the Spirit (6:10-17).

Tyrrell precedes Navone in the title because our book is based on Tyrrell's course.

Final remark: This book was written over a two and a half year period and so we apologize in advance for any repetitions that occur despite our best effort to eliminate them.

Chapter One

Initial Reflections

Bernard Tyrrell

The atheist assault on religious faith calls for a response in our age of the internet, pseudo historical novels like the *Da Vinci Code* and the recent scientific rejection of God by the great physicist Steven Hawking in his *The Grand Design*. In his earlier *A Brief History of Time*, Hawking was still open to the possibility of God, but no longer. Agnosticism, out and out atheism, and relativism permeate modern culture within the intellectual elite at the major universities, in the most popular novels and cinemas and in the music such as the ever popular Beatles' song "Imagine" where the world is portrayed as better off without religion.

Our intent in this book is to reflect on issues common to contemporary atheists in their polemics against theists and most often specific Christian beliefs and practices. Since my doctorate is in philosophy and John Navone's is in theology we reflect in our comments our particular backgrounds, though at times our reflections coincide with one another. Today's atheist's views are constantly in the press and so we do not find the need to outline in detail their particular arguments, though at times we do so when we find it necessary.

Contemporary atheists, for example, Richard Dawkins, Christopher Hitchens, Sam Harris, and Daniel Dennett are often bundled together under the titulus of the "New Atheism." They, like the famous atheists that preceded them, ultimately reject anything supernatural, any divinely revealed truths, any God or gods. They reject anything that cannot be subject to strict empirical testing and verification. They view, for example, Christian beliefs as pure mythology and fabricated tales. In opposition to this view, in the second epistle of Peter, the author cautions readers not to mistake cleverly devised myths (2:1-18) for the true Gospel they have received. The earliest Christians clearly understood the difference between mythic fabrications and factual narratives. Here of course, myths are viewed in a negative way as fabrications or tall tales, but the term myth can also be viewed more positively in other contexts, which we have no need to pursue here.

Hamlet says to Horatio: "There are more things in heaven and earth…than are dreamed of in your philosophy." These words might well be applied to today's atheists in their automatic exclusion of any data that they cannot empirically test with their limited methods of verification. Bernard Lonergan, perhaps the most preeminent Christian philosopher and theologian of the twentieth century, remarks that God is not some datum to be explained, but rather the explanation of all the data we possess. Contemporary atheists are putting the cart before the horse. It is not so much God who needs to be explained by us, but rather it is our very existence that requires an explanation. Such an explanation properly belongs in an authentic philosophy and theology such as that of Thomas Aquinas, who is perhaps the greatest theologian of Christianity, and Lonergan. In regard to the latter some of our chapters based on Lonergan are complex. The reader would do well to recall Lonergan's words of encouragement—"we learn by stretching."

Catholic and some other Christians praise the value of reason and do not believe that it is radically corrupt to the core as a result of original sin. There is then room for a philosophy of God, but this truth needs to be balanced off by the equally valid truth that without the help of grace we would not de facto achieve what natural, rational knowledge of God we possess. Further, in Christian revelation God is Mystery itself and at a certain point reason must bow to faith and revelation.

To say that God is Mystery is not to say that the mystery of God's revelation of the saving life and deeds of Jesus Christ is unintelligible. Rather it is super intelligible. No one can directly look at the face of God and live because to look directly at the Godhead would be like staring at the sun to get even more light. But instead of getting more light one would go blind. There comes a point when faith and adoration are the proper response to the Holy Mystery that is God. But, we must always keep in mind that a delicate balance needs to be maintained in the fruitful tension between reason and revelation. The two actually illuminate one another and support each other.

Our book is based on a Christian anthropology: A Christian understanding of the human origin and destiny. What we must keep in mind as we proceed is another remark of Lonergan that "nothing taken out of context is adequately understood." God is the Ultimate Context of all creation. Navone concludes that any understanding of the human condition or anthropology apart from its Ultimate Context is a deficient anthropology.

Chapter One

Initial Reflections

John Navone

oday's atheists dismiss the truth claims of both myth and mystery, inasmuch as there is no dichotomy between myths, taken in the positive sense, as stories explaining who we are in relation to the Mystery at the heart of all human life. If science is the search for explanation; religion is the search for meaning. Biblical exegetes investigating the meaning of biblical myths find support in the words of Britain's chief rabbi, Lord Jonathan Sacks, "No rabbi ever read Genesis literally until modern times." This compliments his definition of fundamentalism as the attempt to move from text to application without interpretation. The chief defect of today's atheists is not so much their ignorance of biblical exegesis as their lack of fidelity to their own empirical and positivistic commitment. Even the mere mention of the most modest form of theistic belief in the rational explicability of the universe with belief in a higher power suffices to bring down their torrents of hostility.

We meet the empiricist/positivistic atheists on their own ground in affirming that our unique Christian conversion experience of participating in the body of Christ and in the temple of his Spirit is our faith basis for our Christian beliefs, is an experience that our atheist adversaries lack. Atheists ridiculing religious persons for their faith and beliefs are themselves ironically ridiculous in their not knowing what they are talking about. How can you ridicule or pontificate about music you have never heard, art you have never seen, and literature that you have never read? They are unfaithful to their own positivist pretensions, to their demand for the experience of empirical evidence, in dismissing the historical experience of the community of religious faith. Their demand for empirical evidence for truth claims is dramatically inconsistent with their rejection of the empirical evidence of the world's religious communities, representing the vast majority of humankind. These religious communities are themselves empirical data, living evidence of a worldwide religious experience of a transcendent reality that militant atheists dismiss in their preferential option for obscurantism.

The standard ploy of militant atheists is to dismiss religious persons or communities as delusional, as being out of touch with what is real when, ironically, they are out of touch with the empirical evidence of the transcendent reality that grounds the lives of billions of religious persons throughout the world. They are also out of touch with history in their apparent obliviousness to the fact that atheism is only a recent occurrence in world history, when atheism became a form radical chic during the French Revolution. The wish-thought of militant atheists is incompatible with the overwhelming social, historical empirical evidence of world religions. Rather than inquire of religious communities what is the basis for their faith and beliefs, militant atheists reject the dynamic of the question in the quest for the truth of things, preferring the pseudo-intellectual high ground of obscurantism. Bernard Lonergan, in a conversation with me, touched on one motive for atheist intolerance, saying that persons who have not experienced intellectual, moral, or religious conversion often feel resentment and hostility towards the converted who are a reproach to them in their enjoying an excellence transcending the atheists' limited experience. The non-achiever bullies the achiever; the lout bullies the brain; the godless bully the godly.

From the standpoint of the religiously converted, militant atheism is clearly rooted in the mystery of evil; for "The fool has said in his heart that there is no God" (Ps 14:1) and "Emptiness they worshiped and emptiness they became" (Jer 2:5). It is based on the false assumption that the human ego is ultimate reality, that we are our own little gods, in a state of pure voluntarism: the real, the good and the true are what I say is real, good or true, independently of all evidence to the contrary. Self-idolatry, whether of the individual, class, race or nation leads to a state of civil war in which each has become the supreme reality in conflict with all the other supreme realities. Atheists reject the possibility of a supreme and absolute reality by which all others are measured and to which they are accountable; for such a reality would be incompatible with their skewed notion of human freedom. If each human ego is ultimate reality, freedom is reduced to anarchy, chaos, and absurdity.

Chapter Two

Why Trust the Authors of the Bible?

Bernard Tyrrell

We have no argument with scientists as long as they are using strict scientific methods; rather, our contention is with the naturalists who deny the existence of anything beyond the natural. The naturalists believe just as much as we do; however, they do not prove their assumptions. In fact, most of what we say we know is no more than belief. Most of us do not know that men walked on the moon; we believe it on the basis of the media and the testimony of astronauts. Belief, then, is not foreign to the naturalists because they have as many unproven assumptions as Christians do in their belief system. The naturalists are no more able to disprove the existence of God than their claim that Christians and others cannot prove the existence of God.

Clearly the issue of trust in witnesses and testimonials is at work as much in the naturalists as it is in Christians who trust in the testimonials of the biblical Christian authors. To zero in for a moment on the Christian Scriptures, do you trust Paul and the authors of the other epistles as honestly attempting to communicate the truth about Jesus in their writings? Do you trust the writers of the four Gospels and the Acts of the Apostles? Do you think that these authors were sincerely attempting to present the truth about the mission and destiny of Jesus of Nazareth within the cultural context in which they wrote? Your answer to these questions reveals whether you will tend to view these authors with radical suspicion or basically with a positive stance. If the latter is the case, this does not mean that you accept these authors without any critical questions about the literary forms, apparent or real contradictions, style, and the like, that seem to be present in the message they communicate.

It is important to ask questions as difficulties inevitably arise. Questioning was typical of Jesus and the same should be true of his followers, but it is good to keep in mind, as Cardinal John Henry Newman famously remarked, "a thousand difficulties do not make a doubt." It is not necessary or appropriate to suspend one's faith as difficult issues arise. Faith is a firm and deeply graced inner commitment stronger by far than the trust of a married couple who have been happily together for many years. If a challenge arises in regard to the fidelity of one of the spouses, the other will always give the benefit of the doubt to their spouse unless clear proof of infidelity is established. This is also true as applied to trust in the integrity of the authors of the epistles and Gospels.

The strong emphasis in the Christian Scriptures on living a good moral life and telling the truth makes it very difficult rationally to accuse the writers of deliberately lying or attempting to deceive. Clearly the writings of the Christian Scriptures flowed from faith and were immediately directed to those with faith. But this does not weaken them in their basic quest for truth and integrity. Atheists, on the contrary, approach the writings of both the Jewish Scriptures and the Christian Scriptures with great suspicion and mistrust. This is true whether they are dealing with Genesis or the Book of Revelation. When they deal with the book of Genesis, they fail to acknowledge that the intention of the author(s) was not to teach archeology or history in the sense we normally understand them. The authors' intention was to reveal through the prism of the culture and time that God is the creative, originating, and sustaining source of the world and human beings, that from the start our most remote ancestors failed to remain in harmony with

God and that grave consequences resulted from their failure. But, happily, the authors of the Good News of the Christian Scriptures, culminating with the Book of Revelation, sought to communicate that the failure of our primal ancestors was radically overcome through God's actual entrance into history through the birth, ministry, death, and resurrection of his Son, Jesus, the Christ, and the sending of the Holy Spirit.

Anyone who has studied the chronology and development of the Biblical writings is aware of the diverse contexts in which they were written. The majority of Biblical scholars agree that Paul's first Letter to the Thessalonians was written approximately within fifteen years after the death of Jesus, and that the Gospel of John, the last of the Gospels, was completed around 100 A.D. Also what must be kept in mind is the crucial role of oral tradition that both preceded and accompanied the writing of the Christian Scriptures. As Navone affirms, the Christian revelation was first lived, then spoken and written.

Alan Richardson, the British theologian, once remarked that onlookers watching Christians going to their church for worship on the Lord's Day are either going to think that they are poor deluded fools going to commemorate a dead man or they can believe the Christian affirmation that they are celebrating their Risen Lord. Ironically, Paul states that if Christ is not risen, then we are, of all people, the most to be pitied.

Chapter Two

Why Trust the Authors of the Bible?

John Navone

The Christian community of faith is born of the grace of God. Grace expresses what God does for us. Just as when we hear of the wisdom of God in the Bible, we think of how God's action makes us wise, so when we hear of God's justice, we should think of that act by which He makes us just. God's justice, like his goodness and compassion, is not God's reaction to our behavior, but his initiative, quite irrespective of our behavior. God is free to do what He wills, and his freedom takes the form of acting so as to transform us. It is a mistake to think that "justification" means a change in God's attitude without an effect in us. On the contrary, what changes is that we become the locus of God's free activity. Unprovoked, unconditioned, and unconstrained by any other agent, God steps into the void and chaos of created existence and establishes himself there as God.

The mystery of the cross tells of the place where the wretchedness of the created world and the total failure of human resource or human virtue are most fully exhibited. Where else could we see God's absolute freedom to be God, irrespective of any external conditions? And where, but in our own emptiness and dereliction, could we find what it is to trust without reserve in God's freedom exercised for our sake? What gives us the ground to stand before

God is God. The Christian community of faith believes that God has in Christ taken his stand in the human world and answered for, taken responsibility for, every human being, quite apart from any achievement or aspiration on our part.

Christians believe the God whose historical biblical revelation inspired the biblical authors. They do not believe in the Bible independently of the God who inspired it. Such a belief would be bibliolatry: making an idol of the Book

Christian life is essentially the outworking of Christ's life within us, expressing the Spirit of Christ poured in our hearts (Rom 5:5). The incarnate Lord was not merciful, generous, and forgiving to win approval from heaven, since heaven was already his environment. His good works are the expression of who He is.

Our ability to discern the divine authority of Jesus Christ is itself the gift of God. The First Vatican Council taught that saving faith is impossible without the light and inspiration of the Holy Spirit that make assenting to and believing the truth a free and meritorious act of which the word *suavitas* (delight, pleasantness) may be used. St. Augustine spoke of the need of "inner eyes"; St. Thomas said that the principle cause of faith is the inner impulse of the Holy Spirit; Pierre Rousselot wrote of "the eyes of faith," and Bernard Lonergan of faith as "the eye of love." The ocular metaphor for the communion of Christian faith and love with God originates in the Gospel of John: "Who sees me, sees the Father" (14:9).

The effectiveness of Christian witness is caused by the tri-dimensional, tri-personal unity of mutual love (of the Trinity) between the Father and the Son, among believers themselves, and ultimately in that between all the believers and the Father and Son, into whose unity of mutual love they are absorbed. The unity of Christians in mutual love reveals the mutual love of the Father and Son as effectively present in the lives of believers whom their love unifies: "By this everyone will know that you are my disciples, if you have love for one another" (Jn 13:35). The love of God poured into our hearts by the Holy Spirit authors the new life of Christian conversion within the community of faith.

All of this means that nothing can take the place of conversion—intellectual, moral, and religious. The converted are likely to discern correctly who may and should be trusted and to trust them; the unconverted are likely to trust the untrustworthy and not to trust the trustworthy. Unfortunately, it is also the case that people who occupy posts that only the trustworthy ought to occupy sometimes are not themselves trustworthy because they are not converted—intellectually, morally, religiously—and when that happens, a grave crisis can ensue. There is really no substitute for conversion, and that is the work of the Holy Spirit.

Affirming that we achieve authenticity in self-transcendence, Bernard Lonergan makes conversion a central theme in his *Method in Theology*. We are called to the realization of self-transcendence in terms of intellectual, moral, and religious conversion. Religious conversion, for Lonergan, is most vital, central, common, and foundational. Without it, a sustained and perduring moral conversion is a de facto impossibility. Similarly, without religious and moral conversion, a fully developed intellectual conversion that enables us to arrive at a critically grounded natural knowledge of the existence of God is for all practical purposes an impossible achievement.

Lonergan distinguishes between moral and religious conversion because he believes in the need to distinguish between nature and grace. We are, for Lonergan, by nature intelligent and morally oriented. We are not, however, by nature participants in the divine nature or in the inner life of God, but only by the free gift of God's love flooding our hearts through the Spirit that is given us (2 Pt 1:4; Rom 5:5).

More specifically, we are capable of rising to various levels of self-fulfillment or self-transcendence. We are capable by nature of achieving cognitive self-transcendence in going beyond what is merely imagined, what simply appears to be so, to what in fact is the case. To know what really and truly is so is to get beyond the human subject, to transcend the subject that is the integrating cognitive and affective center of human consciousness, and to reach what would be the case even if the particular subject in question happened not to exist. We are similarly capable by nature of achieving moral self-transcendence in moving beyond being dominated by desire and fear, pleasure and pain, mere self-satisfaction and self-interest, into a state of commitment to true value. Moral conversion is a state of self-transcendence in which we become motivated primarily by values rather than satisfactions. We move beyond merely personal tastes and interests to become principles of beneficence and benevolence and capable of genuine loving and responsibility. We are not, however, capable of achieving total self-transcendence or religious conversion. Rather, we receive this type of ultimate self-transcendence as gift. It is an other-worldly state of being in love with God that occurs within this world but goes beyond it, in which all values are placed in the light and the shadow of transcendent value (God): in the shadow, for God is supreme and incomparable; in the light, for God is originating and all-encompassing goodness. Religious conversion is a state of an unconditioned being in love, since no finite object or person can be the subject of such unqualified love. Only to God can we truly say, "Without you I cannot live, love, or exist." This type of statement to another human being, if truly meant, is idolatrous. God alone can be the object of a love that is without reserve or unconditioned in every respect.

For Lonergan, conversion is foundational for community. Conversion maybe intensely personal and utterly intimate, but it is not so private as to be solitary. It can happen to many, and they can form a community to sustain one another in working out the implications and fulfilling the promise of their new life.

Chapter Three

The Affective and Effective Love of God
Bernard Tyrrell

On March 24, 2012, atheists held a unique rally in Washington D.C. The president of the Catholic League pointed out that the big draw was the Englishman Richard Dawkins who implored the crowd to "ridicule and show contempt" for people of faith, especially Catholics. He shouted "mock them, ridicule them in public." The fact that the atheists always attack Catholics more than any other religious group is really a backhanded compliment. They know who the real enemy of hate is and who they must defeat.

The spirit of the above comments is antithetical to the love that is at the heart of the Christian community. For Christians, God is Love and this Love affectively and effectively reveals itself.

To understand the fallacies that we will see regarding the nature of God in future chapters, it will help to set out briefly the fountainhead from which we are writing and that the all-pervasive originating source is love. The writings of John offer the most specific Christian name of God as Love: "God is Love" (1 Jn 4:8) Love has many meanings but the Love that God is—agape—is both affective and effective. God is sheer delight—this is my beloved Son in whom is all my delight. God rejoices in all that is but God also seeks to share the divine delight by pouring this very love into human beings. "The love of God is poured fourth into our hearts by the Holy Spirit who is given to us" (Rom 5:5). It is God's own love that is poured into our hearts and this affective love is effective in enabling us to love both God and all of creation as well. Most importantly the faith that enables us to believe is the "eye of love." It grounds our discernment of authentic values and meanings that constitute our belief system. It is above all the source of our capacity to truly give a reason for the beliefs that are in us. The affective and effective power of the Love that is God can be clearly discerned in those authentic Christians of the past who not only delighted in one another, but also showed an active love for one another. Romans said of the early Christians "see how they love one another." And their love was not limited to loving each other.

Especially during the first three centuries, Christians did not hesitate to show kindness and to give help to non-believers. When a terrible plague swept throughout the ancient world in the third century, Christians were the only ones who took care of the sick, despite the danger of getting the plague themselves. Many pagans were throwing infected members of their own families out into the streets to avoid getting the plague. It is sad that after the persecution of the early Christians ended with the conversion of Constantine and Christians became part of the establishment that much of the fervor of the early Christians faded, though by no means entirely. As we look at the early Christians and their universal affective and effective love for all, we need to be transformed ourselves to be fully authentic witnesses to the power and goodness of Christianity. This is especially the case now that the sinfulness of members of the Christian churches brings a deserved persecution upon themselves as Benedict XVI recently pointed out. If all of us who are Christians really lived the Gospel values to the core, the greatest argument against the new, militant atheists would be severely blunted by the power, goodness, and universal love Christians displayed.

Chapter Three

The Affective and Effective Love of God
John Navone

I n the "The Brothers Grimm" (*First Things,* June/July 2010) Theodore Dalyrymple reviews the most famous pair of brothers in English-language journalism, Christopher and Peter Hitchens. The former is a vociferous and voluble atheist, the latter a reconvert to Anglican Christianity. The former has written *Hitch-22,* the latter, *The Rage Against God: How Atheism Led Me to Faith.* The two memoirs are very different. Peter's displays a concern with his brother's opinions that is not reciprocated. In fact, Christopher is almost the occasion of Peter's book.

The relationship of these dissident brothers captures something of the spirit of our coauthored dialogue with our atheist siblings. However sharply we may feel and reason about our dialectical differences, we belong to the one and only human family. We dwell on the same planet earth, sharing the same Origin, Ground, and Destiny. And from the standpoint of Christian faith, the God who is Love does not love us more for being theist or less for being atheist. The God whom Thomas Aquinas names *Ipsa Felicitas,* Happiness Itself, is no less available to those who deny an existence of the One in whom we live and move and have our being.

The story of Joseph and Pharaoh offers a template for interpreting the dynamic relationship between theists and atheists. The friendship of Joseph and Pharaoh, the man of God and the man of the world is encompassed by the same question-raising and question-answering Mystery. Pharaoh, the man of the world has questions about his dreams, hopes, and aspirations that he raises for his friend, the man of faith. The same God that raises the questions in the one and answers them through the other is acting to benefit the lives of both those inside and outside the community of faith. Without the friendship (communion, community, communication) of the outsider or secular world, represented by Pharaoh, the family of Joseph, the people of faith, would have starved to death. Likewise, without the friendship of Joseph, the man of faith, the secular world would be at a loss to discern the true meaning of its dreams, hopes, and aspirations. The God of all operates for the good of all. If the God of Abraham blesses him to be a blessing to all the nations, the story of Joseph and Pharaoh implies that the same God also blesses all the nations to be a blessing to the children of Abraham. The reciprocally respectful dialogue of theists and atheists, of faith and secular culture, bears witness to the Question-Raising and Question-Answering Mystery that is operative and enlightening in every human life. Paradoxically and providentially, atheists can only help to sharpen our vision of faith.

Jesus' Good Samaritan parable also tells us that God's blessings often come from where we least expect them. Both the priest and the scribe, who did nothing for the welfare of the victim, represented the religious insiders from whom Jesus' hearers expect salvation. Jesus shocks them with the revelation of God's salvation is not the monopoly of insiders; that it can and does often come from the outsiders in every epoch. The parable tells of a God in whose mind and heart there are no outsiders. In terms of Jesus' banquet parables, everyone is on God's guest-list.

Chapter Four

The Fundamentals of the Faith and Fundamentalism

Bernard Tyrrell

Dawkins, Harris, Dennett, and others in their attacks on Christianity would do well to attend to a key principle Lonergan articulates regarding the approach to the study of Scripture and the Christian tradition in general. Lonergan coins the expression "the principle of the empty head." This principle, as he uses it, affirms the falsity of the view that the more you know about a subject, such as the Bible, the less likely you are to understand the text correctly. Fundamentalists (those who take all the texts of the Hebrew and Christian Scriptures literally) tend to ignore the conclusions of moderate Biblical scholars, whether Catholic or Protestant, and accordingly more easily fall victim to the attacks of the militant atheists. It is important to understand the difference between the fundamentals of the faith and fundamentalism.

The fundamentals of the faith are most clearly articulated in the early Creeds of the Christian Church, resting as they do on profound reflections on the Scriptures by the fathers of the church. Ideally, it is the person who is intellectually, morally, and spiritually converted, and is not a victim of the principle of the empty head, who is most likely to understand the Scriptures and the Christian tradition correctly. God is the author of both reason and revelation and the converted individual is one who embraces a belief system that is not in principle antagonistic toward the conclusions of sound scientific studies. An example of where the literalist fails is the creationist in his or her refusal to grant at least some credibility to the scientific view of evolution. Christians who embrace some form of evolution do not deny that God is always at work in creation from its beginning, today and always. There is no reason why God cannot create an evolutionary universe within which God is creatively at work as the various stages of evolution take place.

God is content to let the universe unfold over millions of years, just as God is patiently delaying—though it could happen at any time—until it is the right time to bring about the Second Coming of Jesus, as the early Christians discovered. With this positive view of evolution the air is knocked out of much of the argumentation of Dawkins, Dennett and others against the naiveté of Christians who take the narrative of Genesis literally. Dawkins reveals his own fundamentalism when he chooses to attack Christian fundamentalists instead of more moderate Christian views of evolution, and the harmony between faith and reason. He makes the same mistake when he attacks the fundamentalist view of "intelligent design." In fact, the view of intelligent design, when understood properly and not identified with the creationist view of things, makes much sense.

Inasmuch as the sciences concern themselves with what is empirically verifiable with the scientific method, intelligent design that refers to the divine ordering of the universe is beyond their interest and competence. Questions about the divinity and its creation are properly dealt with by philosophers and theologians.

The Book of Wisdom and later Paul in Romans (1:20) argue that from the visible things of this world we can come to know the invisible Author of creation. Einstein himself was in awe of the beauty of the laws at work in nature though it is a matter of debate whether he did or did not take the next step, which was to affirm an intelligent creator. Dr. Anthony Flew, perhaps the most brilliant, scholarly and combative atheist of the twentieth century, recently took this very step to the great dismay of his most ardent followers. It seems that the age of intellectual conversions is still with us.

Chapter Four

Fundamentals of Faith and Fundamentalism

John Navone

Lonergan rejected the hermeneutical "principle of the empty head" as the sine qua non for an objective or true understanding of a text. According to this presupposition, the text speaks for itself. The presuppositions or cultural background of the interpreter preclude an objective and true understanding of the text. Lonergan affirmed that there no such thing as the presuppositionless understanding of a text or of uninterpreted data. In fact, a hypothetically "empty head" would leave a person absolutely unequipped for understanding/interpreting any text or human experience. Clearly, in this context, religious education is indispensable for a true interpretation of Scripture and the Christian tradition. Dawkins, Harris, and Dennett lack the minimal theological competence for making authoritative judgments on both Scripture and the community of Christian faith.

A basic flaw in their approach to Jesus is their assumption that Jesus' human operations can be measured by our experience as mere human beings. His "likeness" does not mean egalitarian identity. Though Jesus spoke the language that human beings speak, no one spoke as He spoke (Jn 7:46)—for no one knew as He knew.

The measure of the truth of Jesus' humanity is the correspondence between what He uniquely said and what He uniquely knew—the correspondence between what He said and knew and between what human beings say or know. We cannot read our own personal experience as human persons into the unique personal experience of Jesus Christ.

The first Christians—all Jewish—believed that they were truly Jewish and that Jesus was the fulfillment of God's promises to Israel. Jesus was God's promised Messiah. His messianic mission to Israel was at the heart of his entire life story. What, then, led to the rupture between Judaism and the followers of Jesus?

One answer to that question is hermeneutical. The way that we interpret reality—in this case, Jesus—depends on the kind of person we are. The more endowed with intellectual, cultural, moral, spiritual and psychological gifts, the more equipped we are for understanding our experience. Inasmuch as Jesus Christ, according to Christian faith, is the Son of God, a divine Person equal to the Father, He brought to his reading of his Jewish Scriptures something that no other human being could bring. As the Son of the living God, Jesus was uniquely endowed to interpret the God-given meaning of the Jewish Scriptures. He understood them in their true and ultimate context: His heavenly Father. (There is no true meaning of anything out of context.) In that context, He truly understood himself to be the messianic fulfillment of the Jewish Scripture, of God's promise to Israel. No other human being is/was existentially equipped with the authority to make such a claim. He alone, Christians believe, is the divine Son whose connaturality with the divine Father enables him both to recognize and to reveal the God of Israel for what He truly is: the Father of Jesus Christ.

Jesus' self-interpretation becomes a sign of contradiction and division for the community of Jewish faith. Those who accept his self-interpretation as the ground of their Christian faith become the primordial Christian community. For the greater part of the Jewish community, Jesus' self-interpretation is both mistaken and blasphemous, a form of self-idolatry. In terms of John's Gospel, we cannot recognize Jesus for who He is unless the Father draws us.

An analogy for this Christian conversion experience is that of our recognizing, in a welter of foreign languages at an international center, our own language being spoken. We could not recognize it were it not already in us. The Spirit of the heavenly Father poured into our hearts (Rom 5:5) enables us to recognize his Son, his "language," his Word.

Inasmuch as the Scriptures were written by persons inspired by religious faith, persons like Dawkins, Harris, and Hitchens cannot grasp their meaning and value. They are like persons who cannot read without reading glasses. In the words of the prophet, they have eyes but do not see.

Chapter Five

Is the God of the Jewish Scriptures Evil?
Bernard Tyrrell

R ichard Dawkins and one of the earliest Christian her-
etics, Marcion, (ca 85–160), both thought that Yahweh,
the God of the Jewish Scriptures, was very evil.
Dawkins proffers a withering description of the God of the Jewish
Scriptures. This God is "petty, unjust, unforgiving control-freak;
a vindictive, bloodthirsty ethnic cleanser; a misogynistic, homophobic, racist, infanticidal, genocidal, filicidal, pestilential, megalomaniacal, sado-masochistic, capriciously malevolent bully (*The
God Delusion*, p. 51). Is the God of the Jewish Scriptures "petty and
unjust" because He chooses the nomadic desert tribe of Jews as the
means of initially revealing himself to us? If the strict monotheist
God of Judaism and Christianity does in fact exist then his choice
of Israel is not "petty or unjust" because He intended this tribe to
be the means of his gradual revelation of himself to all peoples as
Creator and Goal of their existence, and not because of this tribe's
greatness, significance or power. He chooses the weak to confound
the strong, to overcome human pride and humankind's tendency
toward self-aggrandizement.

Dawkins telescopes all the negative qualities he can come up
with about Israel's God into one paragraph. Throughout this book
we shall address issues raised by Dawkins, but initially we reply

to him in kind. God is not "megalomaniacal" in asking us freely for worship because God creates not to gain anything for God's self, but to grant us the possibility of sharing in the divine glory for our own sake. God is not an "unforgiving control-freak." He is continually forgiving his recalcitrant people for their tendency to fall into worship of other gods and for their immorality. God is not "a vindictive, bloodthirsty ethnic cleanser." In the same passage where He tells his chosen people to kill and wipe out whole groups of people, He also forbids them to intermarry with these tribes (Deut 7:4-7). This inconsistency in effect negates the force of his earlier command and shows a developmental correction in Scripture itself. God is not "a misogynistic, homophobic, racist." He creates male and female in his own image and talks movingly with both Adam and Eve in the Garden of Eden. At root, He treats them as equals. He is not homophobic. The God of the historical biblical revelation loves all his creatures.

Taken as a whole, the Jewish Scriptures are not racist. All people are called to share in the glory of God as we see in Isaiah and other writings. God is not "filicidal," not sado-masochistic." As an example, take the story of Abraham and his potential sacrifice of his son Isaac. Jewish as well as Christian commentators point out that it is the conclusion of this incident that is most telling. In the historical context in which the story is told, child sacrifice was common. The deepest meaning of the incident is that Yahweh did not approve of the sacrifice of a child. We must keep in mind that the Jewish Scriptures are not static, but dynamic. We must see the Jewish Scriptures as a gradual revelation of God as one who is faithful to the covenant He has made with his people; when they fail, He calls them back to the way of righteousness, when they succeed, He blesses them, and always in his mercy He continually reminds them to "seek life" in ever more abundance.

The reader of the Biblical stories must bear in mind that they are not documenting historical facts; rather, they have a didactic value about our appropriate relationships to God and to one another. The reader must also bear in mind the ancient Near Eastern exaggerative rhetoric, meaning that the descriptions of massive killings are not literally true and would not have been understood as such by Israel and her contemporaries.

Taken as a whole, the Jewish Scriptures are not racist. All people are called to share in the glory of God as we see in Isaiah and other writings. We must see the Biblical Testament as a gradual revelation of God as one who is faithful to the covenant He has made with his people. When they fail, He calls them back to the way of righteousness; when they succeed, He mercifully blesses them and reminds them to seek a more abundant life.

Chapter Five

Is the God of the Jewish Scriptures Evil?

John Navone

Investigations of the biblical view of God generally focus on something other than images of God. Many focus on the names of God (*Yahweh, Elohim, Adonai*), the attributes of God, or the work and roles of God as creator, judge, and redeemer. When images come into play, they tend to be those that seem to come closest to being the titles of God, such as King, Lord, and Father, or those that are widely known, such as shepherd and potter. Though we may explore the person and work of God in each of these ways, it is primarily through images that God opens up to us, and reveals something of his divine nature, purposes, character, and activities.

Comparative forms of figurative language—simile, metaphor, analogy, parable—are most frequently used to convey the biblical understanding of God, since through this imagery, we proceed to form the known to an analogous concept of the Known Unknown, from the effable to the Ineffable.

Inasmuch as the community of biblical faith believes that God is the creator, sustainer, and destiny of creation, everything reflects something of God, images God in the fuller sense of human beings (Gen 1:26), or reveals some aspect of God in the case of the material world (Ps 8:1-9). This means that anything and everything can become a vehicle for comprehending something about God.

Many biblical references to God stem from the circle of the immediate and extended family. References to God as father, occurring first in Deuteronomy (32:6), are not numerous. They occur mostly in the prophets and Psalms. These references are mostly metaphorical and relate particularly to God's being the creator, provider, rescuer, and guide (Is 64:8), often with a special concern for the powerless (Ps 68:5). God is also the husband of his people (Is 54:5), implying the intimacy and uniqueness of God's bond established through the covenant. In Hosea, for example, God refuses to abandon Israel in spite of her adulterous liaisons with foreign gods, and makes every effort to win her back (Hos 2:4-3:5). Here God is the betrayed and wounded lover who remains totally committed to the original bond.

With respect to the wider family, God is described as redeemer (Is 41:14), a term with strong overtones of the kinsman fulfilling an obligation to members of the family who require their benevolent assistance (cf. Ruth 4:1-12). Though God is never called mother or wife—understandable in view of Israel's temptation to follow after the fertility gods of the surrounding nations—various comparisons with the work of as mother or wife do appear when God is likened to one who is pregnant (Is 6:3-4) gives birth (Is 42:14); acts as midwife (Ps 22:9-10), nurses (Is 49:15), and is a homemaker (Ps 123:2). God is also depicted as a friend (Ex 33:11; Is 41:8; Jas 2:23). This speaks of the frankness and honesty of God as a benefactor.

The most common image of God from political life, that of king, appeared even before Israel had a monarchy (Ex 15:18), and was used especially in the prophets and Psalms (Is 41:21; Ps 44:4) to express God's national and universal, political, and cosmic preeminence and sovereignty. God is also frequently referred to as a lawgiver (Deut 5:1-22) and as judge (Gen 18:25). These are civic roles. The first identifies God as the one who instructs his people in their moral, religious, and civic obligations, the second on God as the one who will ensure that these are not transgressed or that people are not wrongly oppressed through their abuse. There are other references to God as advocate (Is 1:18), drawn from the language of local courts where God's integrity and impartiality, especially towards the needy, is chiefly in view.

Richard Dawkins ignores the biblical imagery of God's loving kindness, fidelity, mercy, and care for his people in preference for a skewed view of divine warrior images (Ex 15:3), missing the positive point of these images affirming God's liberating his people from the obstacles to their freedom and happiness. He fails to grasp that the community of faith, when employing its images to describe its faith-experience of God's impact on its life, is keenly aware of the infinite gap between their images and their God.

Chapter Six

Do Christian Doctrines Develop?

Bernard Tyrrell

John reminds us in his Gospel that the Holy Spirit will gradually bring to mind all the things Jesus has taught us. This could be read as a defense of his own development of Christology, but also as providing grounds for a certain ongoing development in the understanding of further implications of what Jesus taught us. This leads us to a consideration of the issue of the development of doctrine throughout the history of Christianity. Bernard Lonergan once asked me what I thought the essential link was between the Christian Scriptures and the early church councils. I suggested that the middle term was the Church Fathers. He replied, "I would say that the middle term was 'development.'"

Theology mediates between culture and religion. With each generation new questions arise that require new answers. When we look at early Christianity, we see that it was in the light of discussions, guided by the Holy Spirit, that at Church Councils Christians came to more deeply understand and articulate the equality of the Father, Son, and Spirit as well as the doctrine of the Trinity and the clear affirmation that Jesus was both true man and true God and what this implies. There is no mention in the Christian Scriptures of the word "Trinity" or that the Son is "of the same substance" as the Father. And even in the Christian

Scriptures itself we see development at work. Paul at first thought that the second coming of Jesus would occur in his lifetime. But, he gradually realized that this might well not happen. Paul also called Peter to task for his lack of consistency in his interactions with Jewish and gentile converts.

Clearly the development of doctrine was at work in the Christian Scriptures itself and it continues to be at work ever since. Looking back at the Jewish Scriptures, we see how development was continuously at work there. At one stage, the biblical writers thought that the good man would always prosper and that the evil man would always suffer in this life. Later, with the Books of Job, Isaiah, and other scriptural writings, the inspired insight was given by the Spirit that the just can suffer grievously, while the evil person seems to get away with anything and still prosper. This latter understanding is even more evident in the Christian Scriptures. Dawkins major criticisms of the Jewish Scriptures lose much of their cogency in the light of contemporary Biblical scholarship. But, then, Dawkins and his fellow new atheists tend to avoid contemporary mainstream Christian theologians and Biblical scholars. They prefer to attack the weakest instead of the most powerful Christian thinkers of the day. Instead, as we have seen, they give the impression of deliberately ignoring these thinkers, though some, such as Dawkins acknowledge the existence of these thinkers, but suggest that it is not necessary to deal with them. But on the contrary, I suggest that it is most important to deal with these thinkers.

Chapter Six

Do Christian Doctrines Develop?

John Navone

The Christian community's self-comprehension and understanding of its past is a divine gift in fulfillment of Christ's promise to send his Holy Spirit who would remind it of everything that He had revealed to it (Jn 14:26). The indwelling Spirit, the enabling power of God's self-giving (Acts 1:4; 2:38; 10:45) to the community of Christian faith, multiplies within it an abundance of gifts (*charismata*) and "things of the Spirit" (*pneumatka*) that build up the Christian community (1 Cor 12) and enable it to carry out its mission. Taught by the Spirit (Jn 15:26), Christians are called to be its active agents for communicating the fellowship of the Holy Spirit (2 Cor 13:14; Phil 2:1). The gift of the Spirit permits the Incarnate Word to have a lasting, free, and heartfelt effect on all to whom He is joined.

The crucified and risen Christ promised to be with his community of faith to the end of time (Mt 28:20). His promised is fulfilled at Pentecost when his Spirit is given to remain with his community of faith forever as a first installment of what is to come (2 Cor 1:22). The gift of the Spirit grounds the confidence of the Christian community in the goodness of their salvation as the first fruit of the good things to come in the whole of salvation that still awaits them (Rom 8:23). As the self-gift of God, it is always offered, but never imposed. It is effective only when it is welcomed.

The Holy Spirit abides within believers, as the response to Jesus' request that the Father provide the Paraclete or Advocate for his disciples (Jn 14:26; 16:7) as the guide to truth (Jn 16:13), empowering us in our weakness (Rom 8:26) to know and share the truth with others. The indwelling Spirit comforts believers by "testifying with our spirit that we are God's children" (Rom 8:16). As our perfect advocate before God, the Spirit intercedes or speaks for us "in accordance with God's will" (Rom 8:26). The Holy Spirit's role as the Paraclete or Advocate of the believer combines the work of a friend who frankly tells us what is wrong (it can mean prosecuting counsel, defending counsel, or friend), but only so that, once it comes to light, it can be put right. It is part of the Advocate's comfort and encouragement to dispel illusion with love.

Because God is Spirit, those who worship God worship him in spirit and truth (Jn 4:24); for only that which is born of the Spirit (Jn 3:6) enjoys a connatural knowledge of and communion with the God, who is Spirit. Recognition of our native language in a welter of foreign languages is an analogous experience: we recognize it because it is already within us. Through the gift of the indwelling Spirit, the community of Christian faith enjoys a connatural knowledge or recognition of what is authentically of the Spirit or not of the Spirit in its daily quest to discern the grace and call of God for responsible decision and action. The indwelling Spirit of the Triune God brings the community of Christian faith the peace (Jn 14:27), love (Jn 15:9-10), and joy of God (15:11) in its daily quest to live according to the truth of things. The indwelling of the Triune God in the body of Christ and the temple of his Spirit is the Question-Raising and Question-Answering Mystery, the pull of its future. There is no authentic development and growth in the Christian community of faith apart from the Holy Spirit of the Triune God.

Chapter Seven

Original Sin and Its Consequences
Bernard Tyrrell

The new atheists attack virtually every Christian belief in one way or another. To try to meet every objection would require a huge tome, which is not our aim here nor is it necessary. Our aim is to deal with some of the most basic and important issues under attack. In this chapter, we will concentrate on the doctrine of original sin and its consequences. G.K. Chesterton once remarked that the one Christian doctrine that requires no proof is the existence of original sin. He says that all we have to do is to look at the history of humankind. This calls to mind the contrasting views of humanity taken by Bertrand Russell and Karl Popper. For the former, human beings are basically bright, but evil. For Popper, humans are basically rather dumb, but good. When we look at humanity, I think the truth lies somewhere is the middle. From a technological point of view we human beings are so intelligent that we have created weapons sophisticated and dangerous enough to wipe out practically all life on this planet. On the other hand, the moral development of humanity is so slow that we have not yet discovered that battling one another is not an intelligent way to solve problems that arise.

In the light of the condition in which humanity finds itself, it is vital to understand correctly the nature of original sin and what it does and does not mean or imply. This is so because some later Christians misunderstood this doctrine in a variety of ways. Augustine, for example, thought that original sin was transmitted from generation to generation through the semen involved in human reproduction. This is incorrect and leads to an unfortunate focus on original sin and sexuality.

In the authentic Christian view of things God created us—male and female—in God's own image and likeness and saw that all of creation was very good. God created humankind as free and free from death and concupiscence, the latter of which were special added gifts. In the Genesis story, Adam and Eve are portrayed as existing in the Garden of Eden and as enjoying a unique interpersonal relationship with God. Unfortunately, our primordial progenitor freely chose to rupture our relationship with God through disobedience. Consequently, we lost the gift of immortality and the gift of integrity or freedom from concupiscence.

The loss of the gift of integrity did not render our primordial progenitors radically corrupt. It rather meant that they did not automatically enjoy a full integral harmony of all their physical and spiritual desires. As the Council of Trent succinctly defined it, concupiscence was from sin, it involved a certain proclivity toward sin, but it was not sin. We human beings did not incur the guilt that our progenitors did, but in sinning ourselves we in a certain sense ratified original sin in its consequences and also experienced guilt. It is very important to note that God did not leave our first parents without hope, but promised an eventual reconciliation. Christians believe that this took place in Jesus Christ, the natural Son of God who took upon himself our humanity so that we in turn could become sharers in his divinity. The eternal Son of God was made flesh and dwelt among us. As Paul says, He sent his Son, born of a woman, that we might receive the gift of adoption as sons and daughters of the Father (Gal 4:5). In the predawn Easter liturgy, we proclaim that it is indeed a "Happy Fault" that brought us such a wonderful Savior.

Chapter Seven

Original Sin and Its Consequences

John Navone

The biblical story of The Fall affirms the blessed state of original goodness from which the first humans deviated. In the context of the good creation of the good Creator, the story of the fall attempts to answer the question of evil. Are there two creator gods, one of goodness and another of evil? On the other hand, is the one and only God the source of both good and evil?

The biblical story of The Fall affirms the absolute goodness of the one and only God, the good Creator of a good creation, a cosmos out of chaos, meaningfulness out of meaninglessness. The good God of the first creation story reappears in the Prologue to John's Gospel about the new creation in Jesus Christ. John Macquarrie's paraphrase of the Prologue brings out the relationship of the original and new creation:

Fundamental to everything is meaning. Meaning is closely connected with what men call "God," and, indeed, meaning and God are the same. To say that God was in the beginning is to say that there was meaning in the beginning. All things were made meaningful, and there was nothing that was made meaningless. Life was the drive towards meaning and life emerged into the light of humanity, the bearer of meaning. And meaning shines out through the threat of absurdity, for absurdity has not destroyed it. Every man has a share in the true meaning of things. This follows from the fact that this meaning has been embodied in the world from the beginning and has given the world its shape. Yet the world has not recognized the meaning. Even man, the bearer of meaning, has rejected it. But those who have received it and believed in it have been enabled to become the children of God. And this has happened not in the course of natural evolution or through human striving, but through an act of God. For the meaning has been incarnated in a human existent, in whom was grace and truth; and we have seen in him the final meaning or glory towards which everything moves—the glory of man and the glory of God (Jn 1:1-5, 9-14).

The community of Christian faith believes that the same Creator, in the new creation in Jesus Christ, continues to give meaning to the meaningless, hope to the hopeless, love to the loveless, light to the blind, hearing to the deaf, life to the lifeless, loveliness to the unlovely, joy to the joyless. In his Letter to the Galatians (5:22f), Paul writes of the fruits of the Holy Spirit, evidence of the new creation: love, joy, peace, patience, kindness, goodness, faithfulness, gentleness, self-control. In his Letter to the Colossians (3:12-15), Paul reaffirms the constants of the new life or creation in the crucified and risen Christ: compassion, kindness, humility, gentleness, patience, love, and peace.

For the community of Christian faith, the fruits of the Holy Spirit are evidence of Christ's transforming presence, an effective witness for non-believers rendering the proclamation of the Good News plausible. The social character of Christian witness is unmistakable; for these are qualities/values that contribute to others in their quest for happiness. They are the qualities of the Servant of Yahweh's selfless service of others, challenging them to believe that Christ is risen and actively present in the lives of those who believe in him—the new creation. The goodness of the new creation evidences for the community of Christian faith the goodness of the original creation and its Creator. The same Spirit of the Triune God creates and recreates our state of being in relation to God.

Bernard Tyrrell, S. J.   John Navone, S. J.   47

Chapter Eight

The Virginal Conception and Birth of Jesus

Bernard Tyrrell

Among the key new atheists, Christopher Hitchens spends the most time disputing the virginal conception and birth of Jesus. He develops at length all the supposed contradictions, he finds between the nativity accounts of Matthew and Luke. My contention is that among Scripture scholars today, it is principally the fundamentalists who tend to view these accounts as literal historical fact in all their details. I must hastily add that prior to the permission given by Pius XII to Catholic Biblical scholars to make use of the historical-critical methods, most Catholics, and I include myself here, were fundamentalists and many still are. I think that there are varying degrees of fundamentalism and I do not mean to denigrate the fundamentalists. I simply intend to distinguish them from my own particular approach to Biblical scholarship.

Hitchens wastes much ink on outlining all the discrepancies, which are many, between the two accounts of the nativity narratives of Mathew and Luke. He calls these discrepancies fabrications (I do not accept this latter term). Was Jesus really born in Bethlehem instead of in Nazareth? This is a disputed issue. Jesus was not born of a virgin because the Jewish Scriptures text used to substantiate it actually simply refers to "a young woman" and not to a virgin. I agree with him on this. The Hebrew word used is "almah" and it does not mean a virgin. There are further arguments regarding the historical evidence for a census at the time of the birth of Jesus, the highly dubious role Augustus, Herod, and Quirinius play in the birth narrative, and the flight into Egypt of the holy family that stands in stark opposition to the other Gospel account that has Jesus and his parents returning to Nazareth shortly after his birth. I could go on and on with similar objections, but it is not necessary.

There is a historical method that involves "midrash" commonly used by ancient Jewish commentators as well as by the Christian authors of the infancy narratives and elsewhere as well. John L. McKenzie in his Dictionary of the Bible refers to midrash and defines it as an edifying meditation or imaginative reconstruction of an historical event. If we understand the nativity narratives in this way it obviates the necessity of engaging in mind bending attempts to reconcile all the details of the Biblical accounts of the nativity of Matthew and Luke. Moreover, I should also immediately add that the midrashic view of the nativity accounts does not preclude the fact that certain basic theological truths are embedded in the nativity accounts such as the truths of the virginal conception and birth of Jesus. Also, there may be other theological truths present that are rooted in an earlier pre-nativity historical tradition.

To maintain a balanced approach, I should note that Raymond Brown in his monumental *Birth of the Messiah* does not find convincing evidence of the virginal conception and birth of Jesus, but he does not outright deny it either. He would agree with Hitchens concerning some of the apparent contradictions between the two birth narratives. Yet, there are oral traditions which exist that predate the Gospels and so the truth of the virginal conception and birth of Jesus might be part of these traditions. It is interesting that Ignatius of Antioch, who wrote at approximately the same time as the author of the Gospel of John, refers to the virgin birth a number of times. Brown acknowledges the possibility of a miracle equal to the miracle of creation itself. What is above all most important is to acknowledge the reality of the Incarnation as found in the Gospel of John and throughout Christian tradition. Likewise there is tremendous theological richness in the conception and birth narratives that provides excellent material for contemplation. My main problem with Hitchens here is his usual ignoring of present mainline Biblical scholarship and his attempt to scandalize Christians of a more fundamentalist bent. Independently of Biblical scholarship, it is fatuous to expect people who deny the existence of God to believe in God's miracles.

Chapter Eight

The Virginal Conception and Birth of Jesus

John Navone

The virginal conception of Jesus has the characteristics of all those extraordinary divine interventions in human history which are described as miracles.

Although miracles occur in a faith context, they do not coerce faith. Miracles, always question-raising and question-answering events, have the dual aspect of a divine intervention that is both a gift/grace and a call to faith. Jesus declared that because of the absence of faith in Capharaum, He could not work miracles. Even when Jesus did work miracles, they were only effective among persons of faith who were able to recognize them as meaningful divine disclosure events. Non-believing adversaries of Jesus who had witnessed his extraordinary healing miracles did not recognize them as meaningful divine interventions on their behalf; rather, they preferred to attribute them to the power of Satan. In effect, Jesus' miracles, however extraordinary, spoke to faith and not to unfaith.

The virginal conception of Jesus, the first miracle in the life story of Jesus, spoke to Mary, arousing her stupefaction and bewilderment. Had she been devoid of faith in the God of Israel, the singular event would not have been the faith event that the Christian community of faith names the Incarnation of the Son of God. Two key characteristics of miracles occur in the Gospel account of the event: the grace and the call of God. Mary is "full of grace," full of the divine self-gift through which she is called to give birth to the Son of the Most High who will rule over the House of Jacob forever and his reign will have no end (Lk 1:26-33).

Luke's account of Mary's finding Jesus in the Temple (2:41-50) implies that her faith in the miracle she profoundly experienced at the depth of her being was striving for understanding. When Mary questions her son about his absence and the worry that it had caused, He replies with two questions: "Why were you looking for me? Did you not know that I must be in my Father's house?" The Question-Raising Mystery of God raising questions in Mary is also the Question-Answering Mystery that answers them in Jesus. That the miracle of the Incarnation is both a question-raising and question-answering event is implied in the conclusion of this narrative: "But they did not understand what he meant." It is only after the death and resurrection of her son that Mary will fully understand the miracles that she has lived with since her virginal conception. In this respect, Mary is the template for understanding life in the community of that Christian faith that is endlessly seeking understanding of the Question-Raising and Question-Answering Mystery that is its Origin and Ground and Destiny.

The primordial miracle of the virgin birth and Incarnation is the foundational miracle of which all the other miracles of Jesus are an extension. We cannot have an authentically Christian faith understanding of Jesus' miracles out of context. In this case, the ultimate context for a true understanding of his miracles is the miracle of the virgin birth and incarnation. There were many miracle workers in the Mediterranean world of Jesus; however, the miracle of the virgin birth and incarnation tells the community of Christian faith that Jesus was infinitely more than an ordinary miracle worker. Any denial of the primordial miracle of the virgin birth and incarnation, whose ultimate meaning is revealed only in the death and resurrection of Jesus, would reduce Jesus to the anonymity of countless Mediterranean miracle workers.

Chapter Nine

The Passion and Death of Jesus
Bernard Tyrrell

itchens entitles the eighth chapter of his book *God Is Not G.* Love is at the very core of Jesus' public ministry, passion, and death. "God so loved the world that he gave his only begotten Son so that whoever believes in him should have everlasting life" (Jn 3:16). Paul writes: "I have been crucified with Christ. It is no longer I who live but Christ lives in me. And the life I now live in the flesh, I live by faith in the Son of God who loved me and gave himself for me" (Gal 2:20). The interpretation of the role of the Father and of Jesus in the passion and death is one of the most controversial subjects in both Catholic and Protestant theology.

Once again the charge of sadism by the militant atheists is attributed to the Father as it was in the Jewish Scriptures. We need to keep some things very carefully in mind to avoid the pitfalls of past and present theological reflections. First of all, the Father sent his son into the world to announce the Good News of salvation. Unfortunately, although "He was sent unto his own, his own did not receive him" (Jn 1:11). Jesus' message was rejected and like the prophets before him, including John the Baptist, He was persecuted and finally tortured and put to death.

What role did the Father play in all this? He did not will, but only permitted the sins of those who rejected his Son and murdered him, but instead of removing the natural effects of these sins through a radical exercise of omnipotent power He chose to let these natural effects remain, but only for the realization of the highest good. What He directly willed for his Son was his obedience, love, and trust in all circumstances. Thomas Aquinas says that to command a person is to influence him by way of his reason and will and to obey is to be influenced through one's own reason and will by another Hugo Meynell, makes this observation is his book, *The Theology of Bernard Lonergan* on page 122.

Biblical scholar Ben Meyer argues persuasively that, although Jesus did see his suffering and death as the culmination of his ministry and as redemptive, He still experienced inner turmoil, fear, weariness, wrenching, and instinctive recoil from pain, suffering, and death. This is brought out clearly in his agony in the garden. Jesus went forward, however, in spite of all this out of love and trust in his Father and because of his love for all of us, as Paul pointed out from his own experience of this love. Lonergan refers to all this as "the mysterious and just law of the cross." God chose to bring the most supreme good out of the effects of sin by transforming them, through the lovingly accepted obedience of Jesus, even to death on the cross, into the far greater good of redemption and of the resurrection. In this way, Jesus not only "served as a ransom for many" (Mt 2:28), but He became one with us in the sufferings and death we all experience. He gave us an example, aided by redemptive grace, of how, through loving obedience and trust in the Father, to carry our own cross, our own suffering and dying and to transform them into the highest good of imitation and union with Jesus and ultimate resurrection. Love was the beginning, middle, and end of the ministry, passion, and death of Jesus.

Chapter Nine

The Passion and Death of Jesus

John Navone

The idea of propitiation is not prominent in the Bible and as a religious term that expresses the pagan idea of placating the divinity is not appropriate to the religion of Israel. The idea of propitiation is not found in the Christian Scriptures: that the anger of God was placated by the sacrifice of Jesus. God did not need to be placated. Because God "did not destine us to wrath but to obtain salvation through our Lord Jesus Christ" (1 Thes 5:9), and "so loved the world that he gave his only begotten Son so that everyone who believes in him might not perish but might have eternal life, for God did not send his son into the world to judge the world, but that the world might be saved through him" (Jn 3:16-17; Rom 8:22), and was in Christ reconciling the world to himself" (2 Cor 5:19).

Redemption is God's work of love to restore humankind to its vocation of union and communion with God (2 Cor 3:18; 2 Pt 1:4). It is God's means of dealing with sin and its consequences, and of elevating creation to the blessing that was prepared before the fall into sin (Rom 9:23). God's intrinsically perfect work of redemption is still moving towards its consummation when the whole of creation will be healed, restored and transfigured (Rom 1:16; 8:23; 13:11; Eph 4:30).

In John's theological reflection (1 Jn 4:7-9) we are told that love leads to life because such a life is sharing in the life of God who is Love Itself, and to share his life is to have been touched by the Eternal in time: "This is eternal life, to know you, the one true God, and Jesus Christ whom you have sent" (Jn 17:3). To know Jesus of Nazareth in the paschal mystery, in his dying in a loving self-giving in faith and hope, is to know something of God's life. To share in such a life is to share in a life and love that is eternal. In his farewell discourse, Jesus affirms "I am the way and the truth and the life (Jn 14:6), that is, the life He lives and offers to others is the true way that is life and leads to the fullness of life with God. Jesus could also say to Martha, who knew that her brother would rise on the last day, that He was the resurrection and the life (Jn 11:25), that his life and death revealed the meaning of life and resurrection.

On the eve of his death, Jesus tells his disciples that He loves them just as his Father loves him (Jn 15:9). He assures them that, remaining in his love, his joy will be theirs (Jn 15:11); that no one can have greater love than to lay down his life for his friends (Jn 15:13). Contrary to the atheists holding that Jesus is the victim of a cruel Father who demands the suffering and death of Jesus in retribution for the sins of humankind, the Jesus of John's Gospel eagerly desires to give his life for his friends. In seeing the death of Jesus as his giving his life for others, the Christian community of faith sees the perfect human image of the Father, Love Itself.

Before the ultimate mystery of good and evil and of life and death, Jesus lived with the loving trust and conviction that his gracious and merciful Father would have the last word. The Father affirms his life and mission from the start when, at the baptism of Jesus, the Spirit descends upon him: "This is my Son, the Beloved, with whom I delight" (Mk 1:9-11; Mt 3:13-17; Lk 3:21-22). The marvelous reality of the Father's love is the key to grasping the story of the crucified and risen Lord as the Good News for all humankind. Through the gift of his Spirit, we recognize the same voice of the loving Father affirming the meaning and value of our lives as participants in the life and mission of the Beloved Son and Spirit.

Chapter Ten

The Triumph of Love Over Death
Bernard Tyrrell

When Jesus began to tell his disciples that He must go up to Jerusalem to endure great suffering and to be put to death Peter objected, but Jesus starkly said to Peter, "get thou behind me Satan! You are a stumbling block to me" (Mt 16:21-23). In the Gospel of John, Jesus prays "Now my soul is troubled. And what should I say—'Father save me from this hour'? No, it is for this reason that I have come to this hour. Father, glorify your name" (Jn 12:27). The accusation of Dawkins and Hitchens is that that the Father was sadistic because did not save Jesus from suffering and death, whereas in the case of Abraham and Isaac the latter was spared. They do not take into account who Jesus was. The Father willed to send his only begotten Son into the world as a direct participant in human history through the incarnation. Jesus was not just a Jew among Jews, as Dennett says, but He was the eternal Word made flesh. Jesus, though truly human, was also divine. He was the Second Person of the Trinity, who took it upon himself to become human so that He could actively participate in the history of the human race and in this way to redeem the human race. Jesus had both a human nature and a divine nature, but his identity as a person was divine. As a result, even though He experienced great turmoil in the face of his suffering and death, He went ahead with it because He wanted to share the fullness of his Father's joy with his disciples (Jn 17:13).

Through the original sin of Adam, which was then ratified by the sins of the members of the human race, the union with God was ruptured and broken. Jesus could not take guilt upon himself in suffering and dying for us. But He did realize reconciliation and the restoration of our friendship with God through his free choice to vicariously suffer for us out of love so that pardon might be asked for and granted. Christ, as the new Adam and Head of his body the church, offered this satisfaction or payment for our sins only in the context of love. This is because, as Lonergan notes, it can be objected, that although the offer of satisfaction is clearly evidence of the good will of the one who offers, it is not immediately evidence of the good will of the offender and so it cannot remove the offense. However, Lonergan points out with Aquinas that there is a union of love between the one who suffers and the one who offended, because Christ in giving satisfaction evokes in the offender a supernatural love that was not previously present.

Through the gift of this transforming love we see the full flowering of the dynamic law of the cross. Jesus freely suffered for us out of love and through the gift of new love poured into our hearts by the Holy Spirit. He transformed the evils that flowed from original and personal sins into the greatest possible good. Thus, just as the Father as a result gifted his only begotten Son with the blessing of resurrection, so too He blessed us with the promise of our own future resurrection and with the experience, even now, of being in communion with Christ (Eph 2:6).

Chapter Ten

The Triumph of Love over Death

John Navone

The accusation of Dawkins and Hitchens that the Father was sadistic because He did not save Jesus from torture and crucifixion expresses a view of the Father that clashes with that of Jesus, who tells his disciples on the eve of his crucifixion and death that "I have loved you just as the Father has loved me (Jn 15:9). These atheists do not see the loving Father that Jesus sees because to see Jesus with the eye of faith is to see his loving Father (Jn 14:9). The community of Christian faith sees the Father with the eye of Jesus' love for his Father.

That Jesus dies with a prayer on his lips in all the Synoptic accounts of his death expresses his life-long loving communion with his Father. His final prayer "My God, my God, why have you abandoned me?" (Mk 15:34) expresses both the cost and the incomparable benefits of total self-abandonment to God. Nothing in all creation, not even death itself, separates the Son of God, the Beloved, from his Father. His final prayer brings to completion his prayer at Gethsemane: "Not my will, but thine be done" (14:36). In the apocalyptic language of Psalm 21 (22) Jesus expresses an entire life and death based on the absolute trustworthiness of his loving Father and utter confidence in the coming of his kingdom.

For Mark, the cross is the chief locus of revelation. There, Jesus gives himself totally to the Father in freedom and love. The Father is the Supreme Good of all. Thus, the cross is where Jesus Christ fulfills his service for all humankind. It is the place where He is recognized as the Beloved, the Son of God; and it is in a similar way that his disciples will be known. That the first Christian confession of faith should come from a Gentile, the Roman centurion (Mk 15:39) symbolizes the efficacy and universal scope of the servant who gives his life for all. He represents all who make the same confession of Christian faith in Jesus Christ through the gift and power of his Spirit.

In Luke's Gospel, Jesus' final words are "Father, into your hands I commit my spirit" (23:46), taken from Psalm 31 (30):5. Luke has added the word "Father," that most characterizes all the prayers of Jesus. Luke portrays Jesus as praying with his people. The customary prayer before a night's sleep is said before Jesus' sleep of death. Luke suggests that the death (sleep) of Jesus brings to completion the meaning of the historical Jewish Passover, no less than the historical Last Supper of Jesus with his disciples. In the language of John's Gospel, "It is consummated" (19:30).

Jesus dies with words of filial trust. Luke sees in the death of Jesus the way every Christian should live and die. He emphasizes Jesus' complete commitment to his Father in freedom and love. Stephen, at his death, commits himself to Jesus in similar words: "Lord Jesus receive my spirit" (Acts 7:59).

By making Psalm 31 (30) the last word of Jesus, Luke emphasizes that Jesus dies as He lived, in the presence of his loving Father whom He has made immediately and directly accessible to all. Through the exodus and ascension of Jesus, we have direct access to our loving Father.

Significantly, the "I thirst" of John's dying Jesus reminds us that all the Evangelists portray Jesus dying with a psalm on his lips. The Evangelists employ the traditional prayers of Israel to interpret the ultimate meaning of Jesus' life and death. They implicitly interpret Jesus' entire life and death as the prayer of Israel, of the people of God. In the light of the crucified and risen Christ and his gift of the Holy Spirit, they know that God has heard and answered Israel's prayer for the salvation of all humankind.

Knowing the importance of a dying man's words, the Evangelist selects them from the particular psalm that best expresses the deepest meaning of his entire narrative about Jesus' living and dying in God's love. Psalms 21 (22), Mark and Matthew, 30 (31), Lk, 41 (42), and Jn 62 (63)—all epitomize the Evangelist's theological interpretation of Jesus within the context of his Gospel narrative. Each Gospel interprets the psalm and the psalm, in turn, epitomizes the meaning of the particular narrative. One illuminates the other.

Chapter Eleven

Process Philosophy Versus Aquinas and Lonergan

Bernard Tyrrell

There are two contemporary approaches to the philosophical theology of God that are diametrically opposed to one another and that profoundly affect the way we respond to the atheists. One approach, exemplified in the philosophy of Bernard Lonergan, affirms the absolute transcendence and also an immanence of God at work in creation and the divine immutability; the other is process philosophy, which in its ever more pullulating forms, at root introduces some form of mutability, in a certain sense at least, into the Godhead itself.

Process philosophy at one and the same time radically undermines the basic nature of God as the unconditioned Absolute and robs the incarnation of the eternal Word of its incredible significance. It is precisely the immutability of the Absolute that gives to the incarnation its deepest meaning and kenotic power. God desired to become an Insider instead of an Outsider. As the immutable Absolute, God could not experience from the inside what it is to be human. The only way God could become an Insider was by emptying himself, by becoming human with all that this implies. He was like us in every respect, but without sin. Through the incarnation God entered into history and was subject to the limitations of the developmental processes at work throughout the history of humanity. This is where Dawkins and others of his frame of mind find so much to criticize about the God of Abraham, Isaac and Jacob, and ultimately the incarnate Son of God himself.

Throughout the Jewish Scriptures period God through the Holy Spirit was gradually unveiling the origin and destiny not only of the Jewish people, but of humankind itself. But God did this not by radically interfering with the natural historical process, but rather by working within the process. And the evolutionary, historical process is full of false starts, misguidance, dead ends, ignorance, and sin. Overall it involves a very bloody learning process. But, from the first book of the Jewish Scriptures and onwards God reveals God's own self as creator, sustainer, source of hope, forgiveness, and proleptically the ultimate liberator and savior of all the people. Dawkins, Hitchens, and companions choose to overlook practically all the good qualities ascribed to God in the Jewish Scriptures such as fidelity, patience with the chosen people's failings, and source of mercy, one who loves and cares for the people, but with a very tough love at times. Instead, as we have seen, Dawkins seizes upon every incident and verse in the Jewish Scriptures that involve anthropomorphic terms that portray God as acting in a way that today we would never attribute to a God who finally through the incarnation of God's Son Jesus reveals that God is Love Itself. Dawkins conveniently ignores the historical reality in which God's actions are embedded with all its flaws and limitations.

Above, I contrasted the God of Aquinas and Lonergan with the God of process reality. The latter God is a God who in some sense in God's very reality suffers with us, experiences our travail, and is even waiting to see what we will do so that God can deal with it. If this is who God is then why bother with the Incarnation? It simply ends in introducing new suffering into God in some sense. This doubtless seems harsh. But, God, as Aquinas, Lonergan, and others view him, is Love Itself, Happiness Itself, Joy Itself, Beauty

Itself, and totally alien to any form of pain or suffering, no matter how benevolent this suffering may be. There is no room for tears in a God who promises to wipe away all our tears and lead us into the Joy that always was and always will be God.

Chapter Eleven

Process Philosophy Versus Aquinas and Lonergan

John Navone

Process theology in a broad sense can apply to any theology that emphasizes event, becoming, and relatedness as basic categories for its understanding rather than those of substance and being. This way of understanding can claim antecedents in such ancient sources as Heraclitus' observation that all things are in flux and Buddhist teaching that there are no static substances behind the flow of experiences, the general background to its modern expressions is to be found in Hegelian views on the dynamic nature of reality as history, in evolutionary notions and in the experiential and empirical pragmatism of Charles Sanders Pierce, William James, and John Dewey.

For all their differences, the various forms of process theology generally share a common understanding of reality that maintains what is real is essentially in process. To be unchanging in all respects is to be dead, past, or abstract. To be actual is not to be static substance but to be momentary events in a series of events in which each successive actual occasion creatively determines itself within limits as it responds to its grasp of the previous state to which it is the successor and of its environment, including the latter the lures of what it is possible for it to become. What is actual is temporal: it has a past to which it responds and it is pointed towards future occasions to whose aesthetic satisfaction it can contribute. The real is also essentially social. There are absolutely no independent individuals. Each actual occasion not only inherits the characteristics of the previous occasions of which it is the successor in constituting an enduring object; it is also related to all other actual occasions. The universe, therefore, constitutes a social process where the state of any actuality in principle influences all future ones. In this universe, though, the ultimate power is held to be exercised through that lure of love, or persuasiveness of attraction, which draws rather than coerces actual entities into producing what is novel and aesthetically satisfying.

According to Alfred North Whitehead, founder of process philosophy, God is not to be treated as an exception to all metaphysical principles, invoked to save their collapse. God is their chief exemplification. God is the reality who ensures the continuation and orderliness of the processes of actualization and who is the basis of the appearance of novelty through those processes. To expound this understanding, Whitehead distinguishes between the consequent and the primordial natures of God. The former refers to God's conscious receptivity of all that is actualized in the world, preserving it without loss in the immediacy of his own life. The latter refers to God's eternal envisagement of "the absolute wealth of potentiality," presenting thereby to each concretizing actuality the whole range of possibility as it is purposively lured towards intensity of experience rather than mere preservation. On the basis of his cosmological understanding, Whitehead sees God not as "an imperial ruler" or as "a personification of moral energy" but as working slowly and quietly by love. God is affected by as well as affecting all that occurs in the world. God is "the great companion—the fellow-sufferer who understands" and "the eternal urge of desire" who interacts with the world in "the creative advance into novelty."

The God of process theologians, in its sublime unrelatedness, has nothing to do with the God of classical theism and the historical biblical revelation. Always in flux and with no fixed identity, this God is no more than an impersonal protean force entirely alien to the God whom the faithful of the Judeo-Christian call upon by name, to the one, true God who keeps his promises to Abraham throughout the centuries. The God of the process theologians strips Scripture of its sacred and historical character. Process theologians employ Christian terms devoid of Christian meanings. Redemption, for example, merely refers to a better quality of life here and now in a world devoid of grace. Process theologians assume that evolution is the explanatory principle of the universe; consequently, there can be no immutable God, absolute truth, permanent human nature, or objective morality. The newest is always the truest.

Chapter Twelve

Is Faith Irrational?

Bernard Tyrrell

Dawkins rejects every proof of God's existence. He sees a blatant contradiction between faith and reason. What he misses is that God is not a datum to be explained; God is the explanation of all the data we have. Such is Lonergan's initial statement in approaching the God problem. The primordial name of God is Mystery. Here we are not talking about the type of mystery we find in a detective story. Nor, when we say that God is Mystery, are we suggesting that God is unintelligible. The opposite is the case. God is Mystery for us due to God's super intelligibility. Just as we can't look at the sun very long without going blind so in our present situation we cannot directly look at God and live (Ex 33:19-23). Even though Jesus reveals the face of God to us through his humanity, He does not allow us to look at God face to face in the immediacy of the vision of God that He even as man possesses. As Paul tells us, "Now we see as through a glass darkly but then face to face ; now we know only in part but then we will know even as we are known" (1 Cor 13: 8-13)."

Aquinas and Lonergan both indicate that we can come to know God through some deficient analogy. There is first in a triad the affirmation that God is good; this is followed immediately by the negative statement that God is not good; in the third step there is the affirmation that God is super-eminently good. What is meant here is that there is goodness in God that is reflected in some fashion in created good things and persons. Yet, God is not good in exactly the same way and degree that creatures are good. Rather God is good with a fullness of goodness that is incomparably richer than any created good we encounter. What all of this teaches us in the present context is that we must with great humility engage in any attempt to prove that God exists.

The church council of Vatican I affirmed that it is possible for human reason in principle to come to a natural knowledge of God's existence. However, Vatican I did not affirm that there is a specific proof for the existence of God that exists nor did it deny that such a proof might exist. Furthermore, as Vatican II brought out clearly, we do not live in a world in which God's grace is not at work in all things. When Lonergan and Rahner stress that it is best to present any proof for the existence of God in a theological context they are acknowledging that we need to understand that the grace of God is de facto at work in anyone who seeks to prove by reason that God exists. They are also expressing the view that it is difficult, at the very least, for any person of good will to see the value and cogency of any proof, let alone for a person who is existentially turned away from God to be swayed by a rational argument for God's existence. With the present understanding in mind it, is now possible to discuss proofs of God's existence while aware of the presuppositions at work in the existential context of such an endeavor.

Chapter Twelve

Is Faith Irrational?

John Navone

According to the faith of the community of Christian faith, we are all the created effects of the uncreated cause effecting us, and we are freely and inevitably responding, positively or negatively, to the grace and call of our Creator, Ground, and Destiny, in whom we live and move and have our being (Acts 17:2). We are not self-explanatory: as contingent beings, we know that there is no law of necessity for our coming and continuing to exist. As conscious subjects wondering about the origin of our unique individual consciousness, we know that the consciousness of the human spirit at the diverse levels of its cognitional and affective activity cannot come from matter, from the secretions of the sexual glands of our parents. Only Spirit can originate spirit.

In terms of Jesus' conversation with the Samaritan woman, God is spirit and those who worship him must worship him in spirit and truth (Jn 4:24). Only the uncreated Spirit explains the existence of our created human spirit and our ability to worship it in spirit and truth. Consequently, when we pray, we are not talking to ourselves; rather, we are responding to the uncreated Consciousness/Spirit that is effecting our created consciousness/spirit. Prayerful minds and hearts are in communion with their Origin, Ground, and Destiny.

Faith, which Lonergan affirms to be the knowledge born of God's love flooding our hearts, is its own proof for the existence of Love Itself. This is the kind of knowledge that Lonergan believes the human subject experiences at the level of intentional consciousness and in the dynamic state of being in love. It is that kind of knowledge reached through the discernment of value and the judgments of value of a person in love. Faith, accordingly, is the apprehension of a transcendent value, consisting in the experienced fulfillment of our unrestricted thrust to self-transcendence, in our actuated orientation to the mystery of Love Itself.

C.S. Lewis enlightens our understanding of what Lonergan means by the apprehension of transcendent value when he notes that the structures imply the ends for which they are structured. The webbed feet of the duck are structured for paddles; so, there must be water. The wings of birds are structured for flight; so, there must be currents of air. Lewis concludes that if there is nothing in all creation which fully satisfies the human heart, our hearts have been clearly structured for a Love that transcends anything within this world. This is the context for grasping the meaning of Jesus' affirmation that "God alone is good" (Mk 10:18). Augustine understood this meaning when he affirmed that our hearts are restless until they rest in Goodness Itself. Loving, wise and cheerful persons, whatever their limitations, are the best evidence we have for believing in the existence of a transcendent Love, Wisdom, and Happiness.

Love affects the whole person, mind and heart (intellect and will), immanently and transcendently. Just as love discloses and reveals the goodness and dignity of another person's whole being, so we in turn love that person in and through our whole being. But when the beloved is Love Itself and infinitely valuable, then that love may be absolute, unlimited and the ground for all other limited forms of love. It transvalues all other values and provides a people with motives for carrying out the personal and communal goals that are deemed to be truly worthwhile.

While religious loving may ground and motivate political, domestic, and personal loving, just as moral reasoning depends on an expanding, practical and theoretical reasoning, so religious reasoning, while it may motivate moral and cognitive reasoning, also needs to develop and perfect both patterns of reasoning if it is to achieve its higher goals. You may, for example, love your neighbor, but in trying to help a neighbor in trouble, you may misunderstand and misconstrue his situation and make matters worse. Religious leaders may truly love their people and be sincerely desirous to lead them to better ways of living, but they may also be morally obtuse and intellectually impoverished. As a result, their religious idealism may lead to disastrous policies and consequences.

For any authentic knower, chooser, and lover, to be authentic is to have appropriated the basic tension between unrestricted capacity and restricted achievements. This means that individuals or a community have to have appropriated the distinction between their lived, cultural selves and their potential selves, which may always be further developed.

Chapter Thirteen

What are the Stages of Knowing?
Bernard Tyrrell

Contemporary atheists and their forbearers are inheritors of the skepticism of Hume and the philosophy of Kant who radically limits the rational human ability to come to know reality as it is in itself, and especially the existence of the human soul and of God. Yet, when we focus intently on what in fact occurs when we are knowing, the fallacies of Hume and Kant clearly emerge. There is a difference between realism and critical realism. In realism, we just accept the fact that we do know what actually is; in critical realism we personally validate that our process of knowing leads us to knowledge of what truly is. This is what Lonergan's book *Insight* is basically about. Critical realism, whether a person realizes it or not, is presupposed by any attempt to prove the existence of God and this is why we discuss Lonergan's analysis of our knowing process before we present various attempts to prove the existence of God.

Tell any country bumpkin a plausible tale and the bumpkin will respond "it may be so." Why does the bumpkin reply by saying "it may be so?" Lonergan would say that what this semi-proverb shows is that intelligibility is the necessary condition for moving toward a judgment through which truth is reached and hence some existing reality is known.

To be able to provide an answer to the question regarding why the philosophy of God should be carried out within the specialization of systematic theology and, most importantly, how we can critically ground any proof for the existence of God, we need to understand and validate for ourselves what we are doing when we are knowing and how through this process we arrive at truth and reality.

Lonergan's analysis of what goes on when we are knowing and how through knowing we come to truth and hence reality or existence involves what Lonergan calls self-appropriation. The latter is the personal activity through which we come to understand and validate for ourselves the necessary stages involved in knowing and also in deciding.

In a brief presentation of the dynamic sequence of stages through which we come to reach intelligibility, truth, reality, and the good, all I can do is to offer a sketch of these activities. It is up to the reader to understand and verify personally in his or her own consciousness the sequence of dynamically interrelated activities at work.

Lonergan speaks of the in-itself unbiased desire for knowledge and the good. This desire is unlimited in its reach, but limited in its achievement. We can question anything on the microscopic and macroscopic levels. We can ask ultimate questions such as "Why is there something rather than nothing?" This desire is natural to all human beings. It manifests itself first in asking questions about the data of our senses and the data of our consciousness. The latter data includes anything of which we are conscious, such as feelings and the process of knowing itself. We hear something go bump in the night. We ask, what was that? We can come up with a variety of insights into what the source of that noise might be: The wind, the dog, a burglar? But insights into data are a dime a dozen, as Lonergan remarks. A further question naturally arises: Is there sufficient evidence that it was the dog? If through a reflective insight, we grasp that the evidence is sufficient for the judgment that it was the dog, then we make the judgment that it was the dog.

Atheism Today A Christian Response

If a course of action is involved then the further question arises, is this course of action truly worthwhile? The answer reveals itself in a reflective insight that grasps that the evidence is sufficient for the value judgment, such as, this course of action is indeed worthwhile. What we have here is a set of interlocking questions that are linked in a certain sequence: What was that? Is a certain insight true? Is a course of action truly worthwhile? Lonergan offers five transcendental precepts related to the dynamic unfolding of the pure, unrestricted desire for knowledge and value: Be attentive, be understanding, be reasonable, be responsible, be in love with God and loving. To the extent that we are obedient to these precepts we are most likely to arrive at correct judgments in regard to the realms of knowledge and value and to habitually act in accord with these precepts.

Chapter Thirteen

What are the Stages of Knowing?

John Navone

Biblical travel stories of God present in literary form the dynamic stages in which we come to reach the truth of things. The Bible is a book of travel stories about God and his chosen ones. Abraham, Moses, Ezekiel, Jesus, Peter, and Paul undertake their journeys in response to a divine call on behalf of a people. The self and God are particular agents who can be known only as we know their life stories. We learn of God through other's stories of their relationship with him. The biblical travel stories imply that we come to a knowledge of God from different directions, with particular expectations; hence, we have a multiplicity of travel stories that disclose something of who God is and who we are. (A "Who" is known only through his or her story and its unique particulars.) Four evangelists come to the story which Jesus' life told from four different perspectives, even though they affirm the same Gospel truth.

If stories are indispensable in disclosing who God is, travel stories seem to be the Bible's preferred kind of story. The Exodus story dominates the Jewish Scriptures. The Christian Scriptures reinterprets the Jewish Scriptures with a new travel story of a new Moses, a new Exodus, and a new Israel (Matthew's Gospel). Jesus is the pre-existent Word/Logos who is sent by the Father and returns to the Father (John's Gospel). Jesus journeys from Galilee to Jerusalem to accomplish what his disciples will communicate in their journey from Jerusalem to the ends of the earth (Rome) in the Age of the Church (Luke-Acts). Jesus journeys throughout Galilee and outside Galilee (Mark's Gospel). Even Jesus' parables recount travel stories (The Prodigal Son).

Certain common elements characterize biblical travel stories. Our awareness of them deepens our appreciation of their implications. There are three intersubjective elements in the dynamic of every biblical travel story: the transcendent Spirit, the self-transcending leader, and the self-transcending community. Every journey begins with a problem, a question, a crisis that demands critical attention and a search for a solution or way out (such as an ex-odus, ec-stasy, hope) that is characterized by a tension similar to that of a scholar searching all the data he or she can find that might possibly lead to an appropriate solution to his or her problem.

Faith, hope, and love sustain the dynamics of the journey. They describe the way of being-in-the world that characterize the self-transcending leader and people of the travel story. They describe the dynamic openness and relatedness of the self-transcending leader and people to the transcendent Spirit inspiring the journey.

Home, homelessness, and homecoming characterize biblical travel stories. Abraham leaves his original home to find a new home. Moses leaves a place that is not a true home, sustained by the hope of a promised homeland.

Asceticism and renunciation mark these stories; for there is no journey, inner or outer, without asceticism. Every journey means that something must be left behind, renounced, for a greater good. The journey effects a separation which renders available in a new way the self, the world, and the divine.

Missing the way is an aspect of biblical travel stories. To sin is to miss the way, the path, the road, or to wander aimlessly. To repent is to return. The subjects of biblical travel stories must be constantly attentive lest their pilgrimage become an aimless wandering.

Remembering the way plays an important part in biblical travel stories. The way the past has been remembered is the way that the future will be anticipated. Memories make the future. Only those who remember the promise will be aware of its future fulfillment in a promised land.

The capacity for growth and development is at the heart of the travel story. These stories tell of people who are open to the future and faithful to their God-given capacity for excellence. Fortitude is a basic requisite for every biblical travel story. The wayfarer is not to evade the challenges, struggles, difficulties, and dangers of life, but to accept his vulnerability and to venture out, even at the risk of personal suffering, for the sake of a better life.

Chapter Fourteen

Openness as Fact, as Achievement, and as Gift

Bernard Tyrrell

There are a few more nuanced aspects of Lonergan's cognitional/volitional analysis that are helpful to know. They regard the nature of insight in its various types and what is involved in making value judgments.

Lonergan at the beginning of his book *Insight* cites, in Greek, a statement of Aristotle that when translated reads "the intellect knows the forms in the phantasm." This means that the intellect grasps meaning in the phantasm or concrete image that is formed through the spontaneous integration of the data of sense and higher levels of consciousness. Insight grasps meaning in this "image." Only as a result of this immediate insight into the concrete phantasm do concepts, hypotheses, and the like emerge. These latter emanate or flow from the insight. It is very important to understand that the meaning or intelligibility that is grasped by insight is not yet known as true or false. In science, its basic method involves verifying its insight-generated hypotheses in concrete data. In the artist, his or her concrete insights are expressed in artistic works and their excellence is only known through the process of reflective insights and judgments on the part of the artist that this or that aspect of the work of art is in fact well done. In the case of common sense, knowing it also involves the reflective insight that grasps the sufficiency of evidence for judging that such and such is true or probable or not true. For Lonergan, the most important point of all is that knowing is a dynamic process that culminates in judgments and not some static immediate intellectual intuition or judgment of existence. Lonergan refers to this latter view as naïve realism and his own position as critical realism. The naïve realist is afraid that unless you make an immediate judgment of existence you will never reach existence. The critical realist acknowledges that from questioning onwards you are oriented toward being, but that you only come to know a concrete existing being through the process I have been describing.

We have been considering the process that leads to judgments of fact. But the pure desire to know is also in its finality the pure desire for value. It orients us not just to judgments of fact, but also to judgments of value. Of what does a judgment of value consist? Lonergan acknowledges that judgments of fact play a role in making judgments of value, but that beside the judgments of fact there also occur intentional feelings of value and that both need to be taken into account in arriving at the evidence for affirming that such and such a course of action is truly worthwhile or not.

Lonergan speaks of openness as fact, openness as achievement, and openness as gift. The first two relate to the cognitional process, but the latter touches on the level of value and its openness. Lonergan holds that the whole process as it moves toward intelligibility, truth, being and value is unrestricted. It is open to the infinite in orientation. The human being needs to be open to the Absolute Value. Otherwise, God would not be able to gift us with the actual possibility of reaching the vision of God. Here the supernatural incorporates the natural without rejecting it. It lifts the latter into the orbit of divinization. We become not only potential, but also actual hearers of the Word through the gift of God's love flooding our hearts and we then remain restless until we behold God not through a glass darkly, but face to face in the Vision that beatifies, fills us with a sharing in unrestricted Happiness itself.

Chapter Fourteen

Openness as Fact, as Achievement, and as Gift

John Navone

ristotle, Aquinas, and Lonergan recognize the indispensable role of the image or phantasm in the life of the mind. The quality of our thinking is conditioned by the quality of our images. An authentic image of ourselves, others, and the world implies an authentic image of God—the pure of heart shall see God, because they "see" him as He really is in relation to the complexity of their lives as beings-in-the-world-with-others. A distorted image of self implies a distorted image of God. The concrete images of faith urge us to understanding and call us back from a deepened understanding to a deeper expression of faith. The symbols and images we use, whether pictorial or gestural, disclose a world that is worthy of (conceptual) exploring; and the result of our explorations is best summed up in a symbol that can disclose the whole world—emotional, intellectual, and moral—of our response.

Human development is a process of shedding falsely imagined images of faith and their abolition, transcendence, or refinement by newer and more perfect images. We could say that to become perfect is to have changed often one's images of God and of oneself. Stagnation, despair, and fear are related to our inability to change our images. The imagination can become fixated at a particular stage of human and religious development; or under the influence of fear and anxiety, it can regress to stages that we had once transcended.

The maturity of our life stories depends on our ability to interpret correctly the content that we give to our images insofar as they embody the truth about our relationship to the Mystery that we encounter at the root depths of our relationships. Our images express not the meaning of things as they are related to one another (conceptual expression), nor the self in isolation from the real, but the human dimension of things in their concrete individuality and the real dimension of the human. Our images grasp the self and the real together, that is, the existential relatedness of the self.

Believing, hoping, loving, deciding—all are fundamental activities at the heart of every human life. These activities involve human motivation. Vision is essential to human life stories, inasmuch as it is an orientation to decision and action. We cannot do what we can in no way imagine or envision. In Johannine theology, no one can come to Christ unless the Father draw him (6:44) but to have seen Christ is to have seen the Father (14:9). Christ is the icon, the perfect image through which the Father draws us to him. In the measure that our image of Christ is in or out of focus, is more or less oblique, in that measure will our life story reflect implicitly or explicitly the truth of Christ. Every human life story bears witness to a vision; this vision includes images of ourselves, others, the world, human integrity and failure, God, and so on. However unclear, distorted, or false our vision (or images) are, there is no human life story without it. Vision, and all the images associated with it, is integral to human motivation; it shapes our life stories.

Authentic lives evidence authentic vision and true images. Human authenticity bespeaks a sound relationship with the true goodness of the transcendent being of God, which is its ultimate measure. The truthfulness of authentic lives evidences the truth of their vision and images of themselves, others, the world, and God.

Traditionally, the quality of Israel's life at every level had been interpreted as the index of its truly seeing God.

Chapter Fifteen

God is at Work in All Human Beings

Bernard Tyrrell

We have just been considering Lonergan's understanding and validation of the position that we can in fact know reality as it is. But, although critical realism underpins all proofs for the existence of God, we need to realize, as Pascal famously expressed it, "The heart has reasons which reason does not understand."

The majority of humankind has been religious in some form or other throughout the history of civilization. Clearly it is not because most people came to be religious due to a study of the philosophy of God. This is also not the cause for the religiousness of the majority today. What then is the explanation? To answer this question it is crucial to distinguish between the suprastructure and the infrastructure of religion. The former consists of the rituals, the scriptural writings, the explicit beliefs, and all the other public phenomena that we understand as somehow religious. Rather, it is in the infrastructure that the answer is found. Here, in Christian terms, we experience the state of being in love in an unrestricted fashion with faith as the eye of this love. This state is conscious and at work in all human beings of good will and it is out of this state that religious suprastructures are born.

Why then are there so many distinct sets of suprastructures, which are at times contradictory to each other, if they have a common origin in their infrastructure? It is because the dynamic state of being in love in an unrestricted fashion is, as such, experienced, but not yet understood or objectified. Romans 5:5: "The love of God poured into our hearts by the Holy Spirit who is given to us" is the Scriptural quotation Lonergan most often quoted in his later years. He stressed again and again that the love poured into our hearts is God's own love poured into our hearts. It is not our love for God but God's own love that is poured into our hearts by the Holy Spirit who is given to us. God's own love is without any restrictions and this is what constitutes us in the state of being in love in an unrestricted fashion.

The analysis of the distinction between faith as the eye of love and an explicit belief system is basically that of Bernard Lonergan. If God truly wills that all should be saved then God must through his Holy Spirit provide the opportunity to all for salvation since without faith it is impossible to be saved. If, as many Christians believe, only those who explicitly accept Jesus as their redeemer are saved, then the vast majority of people who lived before Christ and after Christ are damned since they have not had or do not have this explicit Christian belief. Karl Rahner in his own theory of the "anonymous Christian" holds a view that is similar to that of Lonergan, but he works it out within his own theological framework and analysis.

In earlier chapters, I discussed the various stages of knowing and the process of making value judgments. I did not develop the point, however, that the dynamic state of being in love in an unlimited fashion is not a further upward movement in the process of knowing and willing, but rather an unmerited gift that moves from above downwards and suffuses the lower stages with a richer significance and meaning. Pascal stated that "the heart has reasons, which reason does not understand." The supreme "reason of the heart" is the state of unrestricted being in love. It is not arrived at through knowing. Indeed, it is a state that has content but not an object. It is sometimes compared to what Saint Ignatius of Loyola described as consolation without a previous cause. It is one thing to have an experience, but quite another to understand and articulate it. Above, I wrote that people do not derive their religion from a philosophy of God. Rather both the philosophy of God and religion possess at their roots the same primordial, experiential base.

Chapter Fifteen

God at Work in all Human Beings

John Navone

L onergan has presented a most profound interpretation of self-transcendence. According to his analysis, self-transcendence occurs whenever we respond to the radical, questioning drive of the human spirit for meaning, truth, value, and love. As dynamic components in this exigence for reality, questions for understanding seek meaning. But we are not satisfied with just any meaning; for once attained, we critically search for verifying evidence through reflective questioning heading for true judgments. Further, when understanding and judgment are not just speculative, but oriented toward decision and action, there follows the moral question of responsibility. Given our best value judgment of what the situation requires, what are we going to do? And lastly, since actions never occur in isolation, but with a total cognitive and affective context of one's character, there remains the fundamental question of one's radical personal orientation. To what, finally, are we going to commit ourselves in love?

Among the apparently endless possible realizations of human potential, such cognitive, moral, and affective self-transcendence is the criterion of authentic self-realization. The Gospel's call to intelligent, responsible, loving service of our neighbor demands the fulfillment of the radical personal drive to self-transcendence.

Faithful response to this interior law of the human spirit is fidelity to the grace and call of the divine presence within us.

Although self-transcendence occurs in every instance of intelligent, responsible loving, the crucial instances of self-transcendence are those special life-transforming events we call conversions, radical reorientations in the cognitive, moral, affective, and religious dimensions of one's life. Conversions do not introduce the reality of self-transcendence to our lives; rather, they bring our drive for it to the center of our lives. They turn the possible and sporadic into the probable and regular.

For Lonergan, affective conversion is a falling-in-love through which one becomes a loving person in whom love establishes itself as a first principle, pervading one's life, and from it flow one's joys and sorrows, desires and fears, one's discernment of values, one's decisions and deeds. Just as one can live for the good of one's beloved, one's love can extend to the entire human family. Jesus' example of a vision in which no one is a stranger can become a reality in one's own life.

A fully religious conversion is, for Lonergan, a falling-in-love with God without limits, qualifications, conditions, or reservations, experienced as otherworldly joy, peace, and happiness. Falling-in-love involves the unreserved surrender of any pretense to absolute autonomy, allowing God to move from the periphery to the center of one's life, so that all one's life and all reality is seen as gift. As an event in our conscious living, religious conversion changes the data of our consciousness; it introduces a new content into our consciousness, but not an explicitly known object.

Religious conversion is always a graced event. This means it is not and cannot be the product of merely human knowing, choosing, or acting. It is a gift, entirely unmerited and unearned; it is the result of God's free communication. Secondly, it entails a total change in a person's or a community's orientation. It is a complete shift from one horizon of human operations to another that amounts to a revolution in a person's or a community's solution to the problem of human living together in the presence of God. It is a gift, not an achievement. Thirdly, it regards the turning from sin and moral impotence to God, the crux of conversion. It involves, in Aquinas' terms, a motion or change in the human will in which it is moved by God and does not move itself, and it is called operative grace. It transforms a person radically, dynamically, and, in principle, permanently. It changes one's antecedent willingness so that a person becomes antecedently willing to do the good that previously one was unwilling to do. Conversion is solely God's doing. No human being can "convert" another; only God can do that. Fourthly, conversion involves "cooperative grace." As Augustine put it, "God can create us without us, but He cannot save us without us." God helps us cooperate, but our free cooperation is needed. For both Aquinas and Lonergan conversion is incomplete if the people converted by God do not freely and fully accept God's gift by making a religious commitment.

Chapter Sixteen

The Question-Raising, Question-Answering Holy Mystery

Bernard Tyrrell

Richard Dawkins, directly or indirectly, spends most of his first 200 pages in *The God Delusion* in attempts to disapprove various forms of arguments for the existence of the Jewish and/or Christian God. So far we have taken, at times, a defensive posture in attempting to show the errors at work in certain caricatures of the God of the Scriptures that Dawkins, Hitchens, and other likeminded atheists create; but overall we have been on the offensive in showing the positive richness in the Christian Scriptures, beliefs and practices, which Dawkins, Hitchens, and their fellow atheists conveniently ignore.

God is the Question-Raising, Question-Answering Holy Mystery in everyone's life. A philosophy not in itself inimical to Christianity generates four questions that point us in the direction of a proof for the existence of God and open us up to strictly religious questions. The basic form of the question of God arises first when we question our questioning. What are we doing when we question our questioning? We notice our questions when they arise and that they are at the beginning of our process of knowing. They do not come from nowhere. Where do they come from and where are they leading us. We are attentive to the data our senses and our consciousness present to us. If we are heavily biased we simply consciously or unconsciously exclude certain data, which is what the militant atheists do. Our questioning first manifests itself it in our spontaneous asking what the meaning is of certain data to which we have been attentive. This leads to an insight into what the data presented to us means. As a child, my father showed me a stick in the water. He questioned me about whether the stick was bent or not. I said that it was bent. He pulled it out of the water and it was straight. This gave rise to further questions. Our questioning desire to understand is initially satisfied when we actually grasp the meaning of the data. This is how we come to understand, to get insights. But, insights into data just give us meaning, but not yet verified meaning or knowledge of what is. Here a first glimmer of the God-question has its origin. Our attentive questioning reveals that it is through grasping intelligibility in the data of our sense, such as the stick in the water or the data of our consciousness. that we move toward truth and through truth to reality. But, if the data is intelligible it means that the objects of our understanding must be intelligible. It is only through grasping meaning that we can move toward the affirmation of the truth of our understanding and thence reality. But, a further question arises: how can whatever we understand (including the cosmos or universe) be intelligible? Does the intelligibility of the object presuppose an ultimate intelligent source? Is this intelligible ground of all the objects in the universe God? Such is the first question.

A second question spontaneously arises about whether the intelligibility we grasp is true or not, probable or improbable? In asking if it is true we need to grasp evidence for validating our insight. In a reflective insight we grasp sufficient or insufficient evidence for affirming that something is true or not true. If the evidence is sufficient we reach the truth or falsity of our insight. What we continually find is that each existing entity we reach through judgment is conditioned, that is, it is contingent. It requires conditions to be fulfilled for it to be; for example, I am dependent on air in order to breathe. I am a conditioned reality, dependent on all sorts of things. This is what being a conditioned reality means. But, does not this naturally lead us to ask is if there exists some unconditioned Reality that requires no conditions outside itself to exist. Once more the question of God arises.

A third form of the question of God arises when we deliberate about our deliberating. To deliberate is to ask whether a certain course of action is worthwhile. To deliberate about our deliberating is to ask whether it is worthwhile to continue our questioning about whether something is worthwhile or not. We are led to ask whether we are the sole instance of morality or not in the cosmos. If we are the sole instance of morality then we live in an amoral universe and we question whether our attempts to be moral are ultimately futile or not. If, on the other hand, the universe of contingent beings is moral does there not exist a moral Reality that is unconditionally moral? Once again the question of God arises.

Finally, a fourth question about God arises when we question our religious experience. It is true that there are many religious aberrations. But beneath these aberrations some have found that there exists an unrestricted being in love, a pure gift of grace, a consolation without previous cause. Some people will ask if there is an unconditioned source for this gift, a source that is Happiness Itself. Such is the fourth question among these interrelated questions. Once again the question of God arises. These questions are not in themselves proofs for the existence of God, but they are the preambles for such a proof. These questions are questions Dawkins and the others do not advert to or attempt to intelligently answer. But they are of crucial importance in the restless search of the human mind and heart for an Unconditioned, Unrestricted Ground of all our questioning and questing. We recall Augustine's poetic utterance: "Our hearts are restless until they rest in Thee."

Chapter Sixteen

The Question-Raising, Question-Answering Holy Mystery

John Navone

Our questions imply that we are relational. Our questions about God express our attempts to understand ourselves; for the way we understand ultimate reality defines the way that we understand our relational reality. The questions within the biblical narratives express the interior life of a community of faith. They are the questions that the Question-Raising Mystery of God raises at every level in the cognitive and affective life of a people. There is no "knowing God," in the biblical sense of intimacy, without experiencing God as the Question-Raising Mystery that He is. Our sincere engagement with the question is already a form of commitment to the answer. The questions that are of the greatest importance to us concern the matters that are dearest to us. There are no such questions apart from the affective power and motivation that sustains them. Love seeks understanding. Love *asks* all she meets, as we read in the *Song of Solomon*, where she can find her lover. A loving heart is a questioning heart; an indifferent heart knows no such interest.

God reveals himself in the questions that He raises within our hearts and minds whenever we seriously ask about the ultimate meaning and goodness of our lives. God is as inescapable as his questions. In fact, the first word of God to us in the Bible takes the form of a question about our identity: "Where are you?" (Gen 3:9). To be in touch with God is to hear his interrogating word summoning us to responsibility. Jesus Christ appears in the Gospel narratives as the interrogating and summoning Word of God incarnate. God's first word to us in Jesus Christ in the Gospels of Luke and John continues his interrogation: "Why are you looking for me?" (Lk 2:49), and "What do you want (Jn 1:38). To be in touch with him is to hear and respond to his questions put to us in his Body, the Church, and its Scriptures. God's interrogating word endows us with response-ability for the communion of divine and human friendship.

The mystery of God, the Origin and Ground and Destiny of all that is human, makes itself felt even in our wondering why we are Christian and what it means to be Christian. Christian authenticity entails a lifelong commitment to the Question-Raising and Question-Answering Mystery of God in Christ and his community of faith. The dynamic of the question, as reflected in both Jewish and Christian Scriptures, is at the heart of the divine pedagogy for human maturation and development. This dynamic lies at the heart of human transformation in the event and life-long process of religious and Christian conversion.

Jesus asks ninety-eight different questions in the synoptic Gospels. He raises twelve additional questions in his parables. Forty-seven different questions are addressed to Jesus in these Gospels. Of the approximately 157 questions raised in the synoptic Gospels, 110 originate with Jesus himself. Even the forty-seven questions addressed to Jesus are occasioned by him. The healing context of many questions suggests their importance in the psychotherapeutic dialogue of faith and trust. His questions assume the capacity for decision and choice. Many challenge the hearer to a deeper understanding of the religious tradition. Jesus often initiates dialogue with a question. Jesus' questions challenge his hearers to growth and development in all the contexts of their relational life—intrapersonal, interpersonal, and social. Even the questions of Jesus' adversaries show that they are not indifferent and are, therefore, at least in touch with the love that could save them.

The Gnostic pattern present in the Gospel of Thomas, where the emphasis is on Jesus as the one who answers all our questions about mysteries, contrasts with the four canonical Gospels where the emphasis is on Jesus as the one who raises questions for our responsible decision and action, calling us to a new life, to sell all and to follow him in the theocentric self-transcendence of total surrender to God. The community of Christian faith selected the four Gospels for their pedagogical value in helping its members to ascertain and to promote an authentically Christian way of life. It deemed as useless the plethora of other gospels.

Chapter Seventeen

The Core of Lonergan's Proof for the Existence of God

Bernard Tyrrell

Dawkins is the atheist who endeavors to reject explicitly all the traditional and more recent arguments for the existence of God. Basically he considers invalid the ontological argument of Anselm, the five ways of Thomas Aquinas, Pascal's wager argument, the cosmological argument, and the argument from religious experience, the argument from beauty, the argument from design and more. Dawkins considers the latter argument from design as what he calls the "the 747" or most complex of the arguments.

Bernard Lonergan offers the most excellent proof for the existence of God I have yet studied. In the previous chapter, I outlined four questions Lonergan retrospectively (he wrote these four questions later in his life) offers as preambles for his formal proof which he developed at great length in Chapter 19 of *Insight*. I cannot present in detail all the aspects of his proof, which is very complex. I will instead try to present as clearly as possible "the core" of Lonergan's proof.

How do we get at existing realities? We get at them through the process I presented earlier as the way we reach the truth about any existing reality. There are a variety of spheres of being or reality: We say that the moon exists and we say that the definition of the circle exists, but the latter is not an existing reality the way the moon is. The first sphere is the sphere of real beings; but besides the sphere of real existing beings there are the spheres of the mathematical, the logical, and the hypothetical and so on. These latter spheres truly have a certain existence, but not an extra mental existence; for example, we don't see the definition of the circle as a being floating around independent of our minds the way the Goodyear blimp is floating around outside of ourselves. Now when we speak of the totality of existing realities or beings we include all the various realities, ultimately including the Absolute Reality, God.

The nerve of Lonergan's proof is that the only way we come to knowledge of any existing realities or spheres of being is through verified insights. In other words, it is only through intelligibility that we get at truth and hence realities. Intelligibility is the sole gateway to being in any of its forms or spheres. It follows that all realities or existing beings are intelligible. But, as long as we reach only beings that are conditioned in their existence and intelligibility by other created beings we do not reach complete intelligibility or Absolute Reality, which is self-explanatory. And it is only if there exists an Absolute Intelligibility, which explains and grounds the existence of any beings or existing things that are not self-explanatory in themselves that anything exists at all.

Apart from being, there is simply nothing; and apart from the complete intelligibility of being, there is nothing. It is God who is an infinite act of understanding and love, who is the Ground of Being itself and who creates and sustains in existence all finite, limited beings who participate in the Absolute Truth, Goodness, Beauty and Intelligibility of God in a created fashion. In her *Dialogues with God the Father*, God says to Catherine of Siena, "I am He who is and you Catherine are she who is not." (This is not to be understood in a patriarchal way; God could just as easily have said it to a man; moreover, God as Spirit is no more male than female and it is as valid to call God Mother as it is to call God Father.) Here in an exaggerated, but real sense God alone is Good, God alone is Truth, God alone is Beauty, God alone is Love and Intelligence Itself. In comparison to God, we are more unlike God than like God, but in his infinite love God allows us through Jesus Christ to become sharers in the divine nature just as God in Jesus Christ shares in our human nature. We are divinized, but in a created way.

God is and always remains the Holy Mystery who is absolutely transcendent and also absolutely immanent to the universe which He creates and holds in existence. God is the Unmoved Mover and Cause of all created causes. The latter do exercise true causality, but are completely dependent in their existence and exercise of causality on God. As secondary or created causes we do truly exercise free choice but are totally dependent on God in this exercise of free choices.

Aquinas held that God through the exercise of divine transcendent causality is able to cause free choices in all their details. God is also in no way the cause of sin. But, as we have seen, God can even bring about good as a result of sin.

Chapter Seventeen

The Core of Lonergan's Proof for the Existence of God

John Navone

T he modern atheists in rejecting explicitly all traditional arguments for the existence of God overlook the histori-cally most cogent argument: the saints of the Jewish, Christian, and other communities of faith whose lives bear witness to the Ultimate Reality that inspired them.

The billions of human beings who believe in the existence of God did not have to wait for the academic arguments of Aquinas, Lonergan, and other thinkers to provide evidence for them of God's existence; rather, the holy lives of witnesses to the existence of God ground academic arguments for God's existence. The way of love at the heart of all the great religions is the most cogent argument for the existence of Love Itself. Confucianism, Taoism, Brahmanism, Hinduism, Mazdaism, Islam, Judaism, and Christianity emphasize the importance of self-giving, self-forgetful love, including love of one's enemy.

The saints are the holy ones whose lives manifest the holiness of God. In the Jewish and Christian traditions, the holy ones are the friends of God in communion with the living God. In the Jewish Scriptures, only God is the fullness of holiness (Isa 5:19; 6:3; 41:14;

Lev 21:18-21; 33:20). For Christians, Jesus Christ is the holy one (Mk 1:24; Lk 4:34; Jn 6:69; Acts 3:14; 4:27, 30). In both traditions, the communion of saints is the people of God, whose holiness bears witness to the existence of the Holy One. In all religious traditions the saints are venerated as persons alive unto God who is their life.

Philosophical and theological arguments for the existence of God are based on the living evidence of the friends of God, the living icons whose qualities of mind and heart and action illuminate and inspire us. Their "love, joy, peace, patience, kindness, goodness, trustfulness, gentleness, and self-control" (Gal 5:22-23) communicate what the Spirit of the living God instills in the lives of his holy ones. Their love, together with the service that flows from love, is the most cogent expression of God's existence within these living icons of his presence.

God's living icons are the beneficent and beneficial presence through whom we experience both the excellence and fulfillment of being loving. Translucent mediators of the God who is Love itself, the light of love shines in the faces of all who encounter them. Their beneficial presence takes the form of ministering to the needs of others. God's living and loving icons express the Love that delights in the presence of the beloved. We know something of God's delight in and through the delight that they take in us. We know the warmth of God's love through our experience of their love.

God's indwelling in his living icons is a mystery beyond all comprehension. Yet we speak about it, since God has first spoken to us about it: the Father dwells in the Son and the Son in the Father, and together with their Spirit, even now, they have come to set up their home in the hearts of all those who believe and accept the world of God (Jn 14:23). Throughout the ages, the great writers and poets of the Christian community of faith have attempted to utter the unutterable, employing many metaphors to describe the dynamic intimate presence of the divine three to one another and to the hearts of the holy ones. The historical biblical revelation confirms the fact that God's living icons, his true images, are the most compelling evidence for affirming God's existence.

The Spirit is where the Spirit acts; the Spirit is known where it acts—in the minds, hearts, and deeds of those who love it. This incontestable existential evidence for the existence of God—apparently missed by the new atheists—has impacted on the lives of billions over the centuries. The conceptual arguments of the atheists lack the cogency of the existential arguments of believers; they are generally based more on speculative wish-thought rather than on the historical evidence of billions of believers.

Chapter Eighteen

Is God Immune from Suffering in the Divine Nature?

Bernard Tyrrell

In the last chapter, we presented Lonergan's core argument for the existence of God. We know from Scripture that God knows all things, that God is all powerful and omni-benevolent. The Book of Wisdom and Paul in his first chapter to the Romans indicate that God can to an extent be known through his creation. There are certain pure perfections such as intelligence, goodness, beauty, and truth, which are not in themselves necessarily limited to creatures alone. It is by analogy, as the Book of Wisdom indicates, that we can come to some kind of knowledge of God, however inadequate, from the world of our experience and its qualities. Further, if God is self-explanatory and free to create or not to create creatures out of nothing his power shows no limitations. Again, if God in no way depends on his creatures to learn what they choose to do, this seems to imply omniscience. Finally, if God is truly good without limitation then God must be omni-benevolent, that is, He must always express loving care for his creatures, which is in no way limited. Nothing can defeat God's expression of unconditioned love and that includes sin.

Perhaps the process theology of a significant number of current Christian theologians confronts us with the most insider opposition to the affirmation of these absolute attributes of God that exist without any limitation. Why is it that these Christian process thinkers are so insistent that God must have some kind of duality as far as his creatures are concerned? They have various metaphysical ways of coming up with a dipolar God. Some distinguish God's real being from his intentional being. The latter pole is open to in some sense or other to learning from creatures what choices they make and then adjusting divine providence appropriately. I have read their argumentation and I fail to find an adequate metaphysical explanation of how this is to be so if God is to remain omniscience, all powerful and all good. What is it then that is so attractive about this dipolar God?

Christian process thinkers seem to be most disturbed by the classical Thomistic metaphysical view that we are truly related to God whereas God is not really related to us, except by a relation of reason. They want a God who is really related to us so that God can be really affected by what we choose and what we do and so can be a companion with us in our suffering and difficulties and can adjust his providence depending on what we freely choose to do. What I fail to understand is why they do not see the tremendous implications of the visible mission of the eternal Son to us and the invisible mission of the Holy Spirit, which is just as truly a mission as that of the Son.

Through the mission of the Son, He becomes true man while remaining true God. Jesus Christ does not have two identities, but one and that is his divine identity as the Second Person of the Trinity. He is, however, through the Incarnation a true human being with a true human nature but with one and not two identities. His identity or personhood is divine, but He is hypostatically united with the human nature of the man Jesus Christ. This is why at the Council of Ephesus Mary was declared to be the Mother of God, not in his divine nature but in his human nature with all that that entails. God can indeed suffer with us through his Son made flesh. Here we have an almost incredible intimacy with the natural Son of God as He lives, preaches, suffers, dies, and rises from the dead. Jesus truly loves us and suffers with us and Jesus is true God as well as true man. Likewise the mission of the Holy Spirit is a real sending or missioning of the Spirit and the presence of the Spirit with us is shown by the gift of love poured into our hearts by the Holy Spirit Who is given to us. We do not see why we have to introduce bipolarity into God when God is already with us in the most intimate manner possible. To say that God suffers in his divine nature is to introduce the problem of suffering into the Godhead itself and it does nothing but create all kinds of problems. God in his divine nature is Happiness, Joy, Ecstasy itself and this was always so and will always be so. We hope this helps people to see why God as Emmanuel is God with us and that this intimacy is infinitely more than we can imagine.

Chapter Eighteen

Is God Immune from Suffering in the Divine Nature?

John Navone

The Greek Fathers of the Church and Aquinas elaborated the theological concept of the divine *apatheia*: God is never less than wholly God, wholly being, wholly goodness, truth, beauty, and happiness. In the words of St. Gregory of Nyssa, "The divine nature exceeds each finite good, and the good is wholly beloved by the good, and thus it follows that when it looks upon itself it desires what it possesses and possesses what it desires, and receives nothing from outside itself. The life of that transcendent nature is love, in that the beautiful is entirely lovable to those who recognize it (and God does), and so this recognition becomes love, because the object of this recognition is in its nature beautiful" *(De anima et resurrectione)*.

David Bentley Hart (*The Beauty of the Infinite*, p. 167) affirms that the divine *apatheia* is Trinitarian love: God's impassibility is the utter fullness of an infinite dynamism, the absolutely complete and replete generation of the Son and the procession of the Holy Spirit from the Father and the Son, the infinite "drama" of God's joyous self-outpouring—which is his being as God. Within the plenitude of this motion, no contrary motion can fabricate an interval of negation, because it is the infinite possibility of every creaturely motion or act; no pathos is possible for God because pathos is, by definition, a finite instance of change visited upon a passive subject, actualizing some potential, whereas God's love is pure positivity and pure activity. His love is an infinite peace and so needs no violence to shape it, no death over which to triumph. Nor is this some kind of original unresponsiveness in the divine nature; it is divine beauty, that perfect joy in the other by which God is God: the Father's delight in his eternal image, the Spirit as the light and joy and sweetness of that knowledge.

"As St. Augustine says of the three persons, 'In that Trinity is the highest origin of all things, and the most perfect beauty, and the most blessed delight. Therefore those three are seen to be mutually determined, and are in themselves infinite'; that is, infinitely determined as the living love of the divine persons—to one another—to which infinity no moment of the negative or of becoming or even of "triumph" can give increase. Hence God is Love [*De Trinitate* 6.10.12]" (*The Beauty of the Infinite*).

God is the Eternal Now/Love encompassing our past, present, and future. The *kairos* of our graced experience of communion, community, and communication with the Eternal Now/Love who has all the time in the world for everyone. Authentic prayer is our experience of living in God, the Eternal Now/Love which, in contrast to *chronos*, the chronological time of routine, minutes, hours, days, months, years) never runs out. Living exclusively in the scarcity of *chronos*, we become understandably anxious and nervous, because it is running out; whereas living in the boundless abundance of *kairos*—the Eternal Now/Love—we enjoy the peace of God.

Not having enough time, perhaps the most common excuse for not praying, entails a certain logic; for our days in *chronos* are truly numbered. Jesus' telling his disciples to avoid anxiety is implicitly an invitation to enter into the peace of the *kairos,* the Eternal Now of Eternal Love, the Alpha and Omega of all times, histories, and life stories. The mystery of the Incarnation is that of the

Triune God's sharing his "time," the Eternal Now of his Eternal Love with us, the *kairos* of his mercifully liberating us from bondage to the routine of meaningless and repetitious life without him.

Our experience of the Eternal Now, of Eternal Love's time for all of us, enables us to look forward, even now, to the moment of our death as our graced fulfillment and definitive entry into the boundless abundance of the Eternal Now/Love, finally liberated from all the distractions, anxieties, and scarcity of *chronos*.

Chapter Nineteen

How to Respond to Arguments Against God

Bernard Tyrrell

Lonergan remarked once that it is easy to prove the existence of God, but what is difficult is to disprove the many arguments against the existence of the Jewish/Christian God. Here the aim is to focus on some of the main objections to the existence of God but it is impossible to deal with all of them.

Rightfully the militant atheists attack Anselm's famous proof for the existence of God. Basically Anselm argued that if God is that being greater than which none can be conceived, then God must necessarily possess existence since otherwise He would not be that being greater than which none can be conceived. Anselm rightly proposes that this being greater than which none can be conceived must possess existence since otherwise even a fly that existed would be greater than a being greater than which none can be conceived which did not possess existence. Aquinas and Lonergan both agree that Anselm has correctly understood what God's nature must be, but he did not move beyond his definition to actually prove that that being does in fact exist. So, score one win for the atheists.

Next, Dawkins and other atheists attack the five ways of proving the existence of God that Aquinas proposes. Aquinas proposed these five ways within a theological context. With this in mind, there exist many arguments against each of the five ways of Aquinas and so we need also to keep in mind that there are as many ways of proving the existence of God as there are forms of contingency.

First, Aquinas argues from the existence of motion. Motion involves a shift from potentiality to actuality because the transition is conditioned; for example, what was in potency to being moved becomes an actuality when it is moved and even an unlimited aggregate of conditioned transitions does not add up to complete intelligibility and complete intelligibility is required. There must then exist an unmoved mover that though moving others is itself unmoved. It is pure and complete actuality since, though capable of moving others it itself does not pass from potency to act in any way and so is complete intelligibility in itself or what we call God.

Second, there is an argument from efficient causality for the intelligible dependence of effect on cause that becomes complete intelligibility only if there is an efficient cause that is intelligible, without in any way depending on any prior cause. Here we have a cause which is pure intelligibility and this we call God.

Third, there is an argument from contingency, for the contingent is itself a mere fact and a mere brute fact is ultimately unintelligible or nothing unless its contingency is related to a reality that is in no way contingent and hence completely intelligible in itself and this we call God.

Fourth, there is an argument from the several levels of being for the many as such is incompletely intelligible and becomes completely intelligible only if it is related to the One and Unique and this we call God. This is because the many as such can only exist if there is a One that completely explains the existence of the many without itself being part of the many, but its ultimate source.

Finally, there is an argument from the order of the universe which, as an ordered reality, is ultimately dependent on an ordering source, which is not itself ordered by anything else, but is absolutely simple, and hence is self-explanatory and this we call God. Such, in brief, are the five ways of Aquinas that each in its own way ultimately leads us to a self-explanatory ultimate Reality or, in other words, God. We will look at other arguments against God and their refutation in the following chapter.

Chapter Nineteen

How to Respond to Arguments Against God

John Navone

A quinas tells us in his *Summa Theologiae* that the existence of God can be proved in five ways (ST I.2.3). The short passage in which he states these proofs has appeared in countless anthologies aimed at general readers, and may be the most famous set of arguments for the existence of God ever written. No doubt many readers take The Five Ways to be Aquinas' complete case for the existence of God, if not *the* complete case for the existence of God. Hence, those who read them and remain unconvinced may conclude from that fact alone that the case for God's existence simply has not been made by Aquinas or likely anyone else.

This is regrettable; for Aquinas is probably the greatest philosopher of religion in the Western tradition. Aquinas did think that the best arguments that could be given for God's existence are summarized in The Five Ways. But it is crucial to understand that they are *summaries*. Aquinas never intended for them to stand alone, and probably would have been appalled if told that future generations of students would be studying them in isolation, removed from their original immediate context in the *Summa*

Theologiae and the larger context of his work as a whole. The *Summa*, we must remember, was meant as a textbook for beginners in theology who were already Christian believers, not an advanced work in apologetics intended to convince skeptics. The Five Ways are merely short statements of arguments already well known to Aquinas' readers, and presented at greater length and with greater precision elsewhere. For example, he gives too much more detailed versions of the proof from motion, along with versions of proofs from causality, the grades of perfection, and finality, in the *Summa contra Gentes*. The proof from motion, having originated with Aristotle, is also naturally discussed at length in Aquinas' commentaries on Aristotle's *Physics* and *Metaphysics*. The *Commentary on the Sentences, On Being and Essence, On Truth,* and the *Compendium of Theology* each contain further statements of some of the arguments. That the being whose existence Aquinas takes The Five Ways to have proved must have all the divine attributes is something he devotes much of the rest of Part I of the *Summa Theologiae*, as well as hundreds of pages of his other works, to proving. Furthermore, the metaphysical ideas apart from which The Five Ways cannot properly be understood are developed throughout Aquinas' works.

Torn from this rich context, it is no surprise that The Five Ways have been regarded by some readers as anticlimactic. For instance, in his atheistic polemic *The God Delusion*, Richard Dawkins asserts that Aquinas' arguments prove nothing. But Dawkins' confidence is misplaced, for the objections that he makes are based on egregious misunderstandings of The Five Ways of the sort that inevitably arise when one reads only a brief selection from the *Summa* and ignores the metaphysical concepts that underlie the arguments. Dawkins claims, for example, that Aquinas holds that since there must have been a time when no physical things existed, something must have brought them into being. But in fact Aquinas held that it cannot be proven philosophically that the world had a beginning in time, and while he nevertheless believed it did, he held that this was something that could be known only through divine revelation (ST I.46.2). Consequently, his arguments are not intended to show that God caused the world to begin at some point in the past, as at the Big Bang. Rather, he argues that even if the world had always existed, God would still have to exist *here and now*, otherwise certain features that it exhibits *here and now* would be inexplicable. Dawkins also affirms that Aquinas gives no reason to think that the cause of the world must be omnipotent, omniscient, good, and so on. In fact, Aquinas devotes a great many pages to showing this in the *Summa Theologiae* beyond the passage containing The Five Ways.

Chapter Twenty

Dawkins and Religious Experience
Bernard Tyrrell

Dawkins, Hitchens, and others offer a number of refutations of various proofs for the existence of God. We have looked at some of them already and it is far more important to offer positive proofs for the existence of God—which we have already done to some extent—than it is to attempt to refute all the so-called arguments against God. But, we will briefly comment on some of them.

Among the proofs Dawkins offers is a refutation of Pascal's wager argument. This is not actually a proof for the existence of God, but rather an explanation in gambling terminology of why the results of believing in God are far superior to those that follow from not believing in God. Since this is not a proof for the existence of God we will not pursue it because of its lack of relevance to our project. Dawkins also simply seeks to disprove any argument for the existence of God arising from the existence of beauty in our world, but he oddly enough does not provide or develop any such proof. He ends up with a mere assertion and what is simply asserted can also be simply denied.

Furthermore, a proof against God's existence is raised to disprove any argument for God from personal experience. Dawkins shows no knowledge or experience of the profound religious experiences either of individuals or groups of individuals in all cultures. Instead, he wastes his time and ours by talking about paranormal experiences of ghosts and hallucinations and he ends his discussion with a refutation of the so-called "miracle of the sun" at Fatima. Catholics are free to accept or reject any private vision or visions, which, in any case, are not strict proofs for the existence of God.

Dawkins also tries to disprove any proof for the existence of God through the Bible. Here again we think we have a case where the lack of any conscious personal experience of the concrete richness of biblical texts on the part of Dawkins and others fatally undermines their objections. Finally, we come to the major objection of Dawkins and other atheists to any argument for the existence of God based on evidence of design in the universe. All of the atheists we are studying hold that evolution basically eliminates any divine Designer. This is a tricky area because of objections from many Christians against any type of evolution. Various Christian scholars, however, accept the basic fact of evolution, but they clearly distinguish their theories from Darwinism in its pure form. Shortly, we will deal with a modified version of evolution acceptable to a considerable number of Christian scholars and other religious thinkers as well.

Chapter Twenty

Dawkins and Religious Experience

John Navone

When speaking of how God is known, Christian thinkers favored the metaphor of seeing, not hearing. Beauty is the corollary of seeing. In Scriptures many of the key terms used of God's self-disclosure, words such as *glory, splendor, light, image,* and *face,* have to do with the delight of the eye in the beauty of the divine excellence. The psalmist wrote, "One thing I asked of the Lord…that I will behold the beauty of the Lord" (Ps 27:4). As early as the second century the apologist Athenagoras of Athens included the term *beauty* in his list of words depicting God. The God we set before you, he says, is encompassed by indescribable light, beauty, spirit, and power. In his commentary on the *Song of Songs,* Origen wrote that "the soul is moved by heavenly love and longing when it beholds the beauty and comeliness of the Word of God." God's self-revelation is no less experienced from the perspective of its ineffable beauty as well as of its truth and goodness.

God created the universe, as Aquinas affirms (*In Div. Nom.,* c.4, lect.5, n.349), to make it beautiful, to make it beautiful for Godself by reflecting God's own beauty. Out of love for the beauty of God's own true goodness, God gives existence to everything, and moves and conserves everything. Beauty Itself (God) intends everything to become beautiful within the fullness of its own true goodness. Insofar as God as Happiness Itself (*Summa Theologiae* I-II, q.3, a.2) knows God's truth, loves God's goodness, and delights in/enjoys God's true goodness, God's creating the universe to be beautiful means that God has created it to be delightful/enjoyable.

God sees what God has made, and it is good because God sees it and sees it as good. God's vision/love/delight is not a response to created truth/goodness/beauty; it is the cause of their truth/goodness/beauty. Belief that God is the Creator of all things is the basis for affirming the truth (knowability) and goodness (lovability) and beauty (delightfulness) of all things inasmuch as the Creator knows what He is creating, loves what He is creating, and enjoys what He is creating. Edward Feser, in his book, *Aquinas*, (Oxford, 2009, p 88) notes that for Aquinas the claim that God created the world is more like the minstrel making his music than the blacksmith who has made a shoe; that is to say, creation is an ongoing activity rather than a once-and-for-all event. While the shoe might continue to exist even if the blacksmith dies, the music necessarily stops when the minstrel stops playing, and the world would necessarily go out of existence if God stopped creating it.

Splendor formae, as an aspect of beauty, can be understood within the context of the biblical revelation. We reflect the beauty of God's true goodness when we *conform* to it. Because God's will for us is always God's love for us, our conformity reflects the beauty of God's love for us, the love that makes us lovely. Self-will in opposition to God's will/love for us is a *deformation/deformity* (ugliness) of what had been created as a true image and likeness of Beauty Itself. Jesus Christ saves the world by transforming the deformed, by transfiguring the disfigured, through the gift of his Holy Spirit of love. The triune God's self-gift, the Holy Spirit of the Father and of the Son enables us to reflect the beauty of God's true goodness.

Joy/delight always accompanies the experience of beauty. The beautiful is delightful. That joy which this world can neither give nor take away from us, analogously accompanies our experience of the beautiful. The delight/joy that the Father has in beholding the Beloved Son in Mark's accounts of Jesus baptism and transfiguration implies that the beauty of the Son transcends merely human beauty. Similarly, the joy that Jesus has in his Father implies that his experience of beauty transcends time and space.

The Good Shepherd metaphor in John's Gospel implies the transforming impact of God's beauty in human life. *Kalos*, in Greek, is both the word for "beautiful" and "good" in describing the beauty of Jesus' love in laying down his life for his sheep and the goodness of that life for them (10:11). Jesus, like God, the shepherd of Israel, leads, draws, attracts, unites, and sustains his sheep. The splendor of the Beautiful/Good Shepherd on the cross will draw all persons to himself (12:32). The beauty of God's self-giving love for us in the crucified and risen Christ saves/transforms us by drawing us to itself. This is the context for Dostoyevsky's affirmation that "Beauty saves the world." This is the captivating and liberating power that decenters its beholders from themselves, drawing them beyond themselves to communion with Beauty/Love/Life/Happiness Itself. Knowing the beauty of God transcends every conceptual proof for the existence of God.

For Plato, Joseph Ratzinger wrote in *The Spirit of the Liturgy*, "the category of the beautiful had been definitive, the beautiful, and the good, ultimately, the beautiful and God, coincide. Through the appearance of the beautiful we are wounded in our innermost being, and that wound grips us and takes us beyond ourselves; it stirs longing into flight and moves us towards the truly Beautiful."

Chapter Twenty-One

Proofs for the Existence of God
Bernard Tyrrell

The cosmological proof for the existence of God needs further development beyond what we have presented so far. Apart from Lonergan's proof for the existence of God, Norris Clarke has also worked out a good explanation of the cosmological argument. It is important to deal with this cosmological argument before we tackle the theory of evolution and so we are going to draw on Clarke's argument in an abbreviated fashion. Clarke should not be blamed for any flaws in the argument since this presentation involves a creative adaptation of aspects of his argument.

Before we consider the cosmological argument more closely, it fits in here to consider Stephen Hawking's view of the cosmos (universe) and its origin. As I indicated earlier, Hawking has recently changed his hypothesis from one which is in principle open to the existence of God to his present hypothesis that excludes the possibility of the existence of God. Hawking argues that it is gravity in a certain way that brings about the universe. Basically, Hawking is arguing that gravity, which is a material and not a spiritual force, is interrelated with the universe in such a way that it does not enjoy radical independence from the cosmos. This means that it is in itself a part of the universe, even though it might be primordially the initial element in some sense in the material cosmos. He is not addressing the issue of a radical coming into being from nothing. As the philosophical adage has it, "ex nihilo nihil fit" or in awkward translation, "out of nothing nothing comes" and hence he is not really talking about creation out of absolutely nothing, which is the common philosophical/theological understanding of the monotheistic religions concerning the origin of the cosmos.

The basic question is why do beings exist and why do they exist at all in the way they do exist? What is the necessary and sufficient explanation for why they exist at all? Atheists would say that the world as a whole just exists and that's it. The scientist must begin with subject matter that exists, but in principle the scientist cannot use his own methods to prove the existence of his own subject matter. Rather science is limited to its own method of verifying hypotheses in data and these empirical hypotheses are necessarily subject to the empirical principle of falsifiability; for example, the Big Bang is presently accepted as the beginning of the universe as we know it. But science cannot exclude the possibility that there may be another better hypothesis, one that even falsifies the first, in the offing.

Human beings depend on all sorts of factors for them to exist. They are not self-sufficient. The same may be said of animals, plants, molecules, atoms, primordial particles that make up atoms, elementary particles, and the like. Even the latter cannot exist alone, but must be joined with two or three others. There is nothing we have found in the universe of our experience that exists independently of anything else and so we live in a conditioned universe on the macro and micro levels. Thus, nothing in this universe so far has been shown to be non-dependent on anything else and so whether taken individually as parts or together as the whole that constitutes our universe we see that everything is shot through with contingency and dependence on other beings and hence our universe is not in any of its parts or all of them together self-explanatory.

It also does not work to say that conditioned A depends on conditioned B that in turn depends on another conditioned being for its causation since even in an infinite regress, unless a non-conditioned being is posited as the source of the chain of conditioned realities, the whole chain is unintelligible and as Aquinas and Lonergan both say, what is not in itself per se intelligible cannot be. This same statement may be made even regarding chaos theory because unless it is intelligible we would not even be able to think or talk about it at all.

Some argue that causal dependence may be circular, i.e. A depends on B and B depends on C and C in turn depends on A. This argument does not work because it is manifestly contradictory for the same being to be at the same time prior and posterior to another being in the same order of dependence.

Here we are led to the further question about whether a being that is self-sufficient for its own existence is infinite in perfection, that is, it possesses in a strictly unrestricted way the qualitative fullness of all perfections. If we suppose for the moment that this being is finite then this would mean that the positive qualities it possesses exist in a limited fashion and so there can always exist some further limited form of these perfections which may be higher, but still limited. Only a being that possesses the fullness of positive perfections in an unlimited way can be the source of beings whose positive qualities exist in a limited way. Among the unlimited positive qualities of this supreme Ultimate being are love, intelligence, goodness, power, beauty and, of course, above all existence.

Chapter Twenty-One

Proofs for the Existence of God

John Navone

Edward Feser (*Aquinas*, Oxford, 2009, p. 90) notes that the proof from the contingency of the world starts from the fact that there are in the natural order of things for which it is possible either to exist or not exist, as is evident from the fact that they are generated or corrupted, coming into being and passing away. But, as Aquinas affirms, "that which is possible not to be at some time is not" (ST I.2.3); that is to say, if it is possible for something not to exist, then at some time it will not exist. "Therefore, if everything is possible not to be, then at one time there could have been nothing in existence" (ST I.2.3.). Now, if there ever were a time when nothing existed, then nothing would exist now, because "that which does not exist only begins to exist by something already existing" (ST I.2.3), so that if there was nothing in existence at some point in the past there would have been no way for anything new to be brought into existence. But since it would be absurd to hold that nothing exists now, it follows (given the assumption that everything that exists is merely possible leads to this absurdity) that not everything that exists is merely possible, that is, capable of existing or not existing; and, therefore "there must exist something the existence of which is necessary" (ST I.2.3.). Now "every necessary thing either has its necessity caused by another, or not" (ST

I.2.3). But it is impossible to go on to infinity in a series of necessary things that get their necessity from another; therefore, there must be something "having of itself its own necessity, and not receiving it from another, but rather causing in others their necessity" (ST I.2.3), and this is what we call God (E. Feser, *Aquinas*, p. 91).

Aquinas does not think that a necessary being having its necessity of itself is one whose essence "includes" existence, as if its existence were simply one attribute it had alongside others. Rather, he thinks of it as something which just *is* subsistent existence, Being Itself, rather than "a being" among other beings, and as something absolutely simple or non-composite in which no distinctions can be drawn between its various attributes.

Aquinas does not argue to the existence of God from the claim that everything has a cause, nor does he argue that the universe had a beginning and that God must have been the cause of that beginning. Rather, as Edward Feser remarks in *The Last Superstition: A Refutation of the New Atheism*, his aim is to show that given that there are in fact some causes of various sorts, the nature of cause and effect entails that God is necessary as an uncaused cause of the universe even if we assume that the universe has always existed and thus had no beginning. The argument is not that the world would not have got started if God had not knocked down the first domino at some point in the distant past; it is that it would not exist *here and now,* and at every moment, sustaining it in being, change, and goal-directedness.

Chapter Twenty-Two

Causality and Order

Bernard Tyrrell

We can step back and take as our starting point the complete system of our material cosmos taken as a whole. The cosmos is as a whole a limited, determinate system whose constants are clearly and precisely limited; for example, the speed of light, the force of gravity, and the like. But a new question arises that asks "Why this particular determinate universe and not another?" The system itself can provide no answer. There is no scientific way of explaining the brute fact of the existing universe and what is a sheer brute fact lacks intelligibility and so cannot be. What we are using here is a pure metaphysical argument and no changes or progress in the content of the sciences can or will ever rebut this.

As we have already noted, Hawking in his *Grand Design* provides us with an argument that attempts to show how the universe came into existence from "nothing" but the "nothing" Hawking is speaking of is not the "nothing" of which theistic faith and metaphysics speaks. Hawking's "scientific" hypothesis in the Grand Design begs the question because he uses contingent forces such as gravity to validate his hypothesis. Hawking is actually venturing into metaphysics, which can reach certitudes, which hypotheses

Bernard Tyrrell, S. J.   John Navone, S. J.

of physics can never reach given the limitations of the scientific method as such.

The ancient argument from order and design is the argument Aquinas calls the most widespread argument for the existence of God in all times and cultures. Clarke agrees with Aquinas regarding this argument. In the present period of evolutionary science, however, this proof does require certain adaptations. We have today the argument from "intelligent design," which muddies this whole discussion and is not to be facilely identified with the proof Aquinas is talking about. The distinction between scientific explanation and "the intelligent design" approach does not seem to recognize that science can never in the light of its own methods prove that an Intelligent Designer actually exists and so it should not and cannot be taught in a strictly scientific course such as physics, chemistry, biology, and such. We will deal with evolution next.

As a preview, however, we might look at Dawkins argument that since the universe is so complex, if indeed there was a God, which there is not, this God would be incredibly complicated and so would have to have undergone an even more complicated evolutionary development. The classic arguments for the existence of God all conclude that God is Spirit, God has no parts, and God is simple and one in the most profound sense of those words. If ever there was an argument that begged the question it is this one. You would use one type of evolution to prove the validity of another type of evolution, which could go on ad infinitum.

We have already somewhat touched upon the argument for order or design in the universe. But, I will give a brief example of the three metaphysical causes Aquinas, Lonergan, and Clarke all embrace, among which is included exemplary causality. First there is the argument for final causality; this is followed by the argument for exemplary causality and finally the argument for efficient causality. To begin I simply present an example of final causality. When I want to get to the store, I experience final causality. My reason for going to the store is the final cause or purpose that motivates me as the good or end I wish to achieve. The second cause is exemplary causality. I need to have a plan about how I can best get to the store. Finally, there is efficient causality. This is exercised when I get in the car, drive to the store, and pick out what I need. The final cause is the first in intention but the last in execution. I need a purpose to reach the end or good or goal I desire. God cannot create apart from a final causality. He has to desire to freely share his goodness with others, not for his sake but for us. This is what motivates him to create. Second, if God is going to create He needs a plan. The plan is what we mean by exemplary causality. Finally, as we have seen, there is efficient causality. God freely creates and this is what we mean by his efficient causality. We need to keep these causes in mind when we discuss evolution as we are now going to do.

Chapter Twenty-Two

Causality and Order

John Navone

We live to know more than ourselves, even though "know thyself" remains our first duty. We delight in knowing. We often notice that when we begin a project or read a book, time passes unnoticed, almost as if we stand outside of time. Everything *that is* we find not merely admirable, but something that incites us, something that makes us realize that the world is more than ourselves yet also includes us in some order we seek to clarify.

Aquinas deals with the question whether the truth is a special virtue (II-II, 109, 2). The question arises because the truth is primarily a question of the intellect, of both the intellectual and practical virtues. On the other hand, whether we act to tell the truth when the occasion arises indicates a moral attitude. Thus, the moral virtue of truth-telling means not only that we know the truth that we speak, but that we speak it, attest to it. The human good consists in using our minds properly.

Aquinas then cites Augustine, who said the good consists in "order." The special character of the good consists in "order." The special character of the good is the manifestation of a definite order. There is a special order in which our exterior words or acts are duly ordained to something, as a sign to that which is signified within us. And this is what perfects us through order—that is, we manifest in our words and acts in the order of a thing that is. The good of our minds is to know and manifest this order.

There are various kinds of order we might encounter. The mind wants to know that this thing is not that thing. It strives to distinguish. It seeks to know and manifest the difference among things, including human things. The human mind implicitly assumes there is order among things because it looks for it. We have to be talked out of order with very subtle arguments or proofs to think that there is no order or that the only *order* that exists is the one we impose on things.

The great Church Doctor Athanasius, in his "Discourse against the Pagans," stated what is no doubt the common view.

It is right that creation should exist as He made it and as we see it happening, because this is his will, which no one would deny. For if the movement of the universe was irrational, and the world rolled on in random fashion, one would be justified in disbelieving what we say. But if the world is founded on reason, wisdom, and science, and is filled with orderly beauty, then it must owe its origin and order to none other.

The order is a willed order. It is not irrational, though its rationality is not a manmade rationality. This order does not mean that human minds cannot know something of it, beginning from *what is*. The cosmos does not roll on in a random fashion.

There remain, of course, those who find no order in reason or reality. However, the fact is that the mind is made, not by itself, to know *what is*, and as best as it can, does so. We want to know, we have a longing to know the order of things, and the various orders within this general order, which as Socrates said, it is made to be ordered by Mind.

Chapter Twenty-Three

The Origin of the Cosmos
Bernard Tyrrell

Dawkins, Dennett, Hitchens, and Harris all use the theory of evolution to disprove some basic Christian claims. Rightly, as we see it, their objections are valid if an individual is a fundamentalist who basically rejects any theory of evolution. However, not all Christians reject evolution when the latter is properly understood within a theistic context.

What is a theistic context? It is the opposite of a deistic context. Anthony Flew, perhaps the most notorious atheist of the twentieth century, recently converted to a theistic worldview, but not to a Christian worldview. Although particularly sympathetic to Christian claims, due in large part to his dialogues with N.T. Wright, the well-known British evangelical Anglican Biblical scholar, he finds the problem of evil too great for him to adopt a revelational religion. Deism is basically the view that there does exist an intelligent being, distinct from created reality, which brought the universe into existence and then left it to its own devices. Catholic Christians, however, and some other Christians believe in a personal God, who brings the world into existence, holds it in existence, is the first agent of every event, every development, and every emergent reality, and applies every finite agent to its operation.

There are a few major preambles to the discussion of the theory of evolution, which it is most important to mention and which Lonergan proposes. God then in the present specific context does not in his planning of the created universe put it together piece by piece; rather, as an infinite act of understanding, God understands every possible universe in all its details, including specific free choices and He freely chooses to create one of these. Since there are no real distinctions in God between his omniscience, omnipotence, and freedom it is by the same act that God knows, loves and delights in himself that He freely chooses to bring into existence the present created universe of our experience.

What is most important to keep in mind is the nature of God's and our own actions as efficient causes. Hume understood efficient causality as a sequence of before/after events. Aquinas and Lonergan understood efficient causality and what it causes as simultaneous events. There is no time lapse between them, for example, the fire cooks the steak, but the steak only exists as cooking as long as the fire continues causing. Lonergan defines efficient causality as the intelligible dependence of B on A. This is why the universe only exists as long as God is creating it, which radically separates this position from that of deism.

Another crucial point to understand is that there is no contradiction involved between the two propositions that God knows, wills, and creates this particular free act and the proposition that this free act exists. This is because the two propositions are verified by the same contingent reality, that is, the existence of the free act. In other words, where two propositions require the same contingent term for their validity the one proposition does not necessitate the other proposition, for example, if Socrates sits then he necessarily sits, but he need not have sat at all. For centuries theologians have argued about how God can create a free act without necessitating the free act and hence becoming involved in a contradiction. The Dominicans and the Jesuits got into such a rancorous debate about this issue that it was going nowhere and the pope finally ordered the two to stop arguing about this. I don't think that papal intervention is the best way of solving an argument but this is what in fact happened. For additional support for his position Lonergan appeals to Aquinas who articulates the theorem of divine transcendence. God as the Absolute transcends the orders of created necessity and freedom.

This chapter is doubtless the most demanding in its metaphysical argumentation and I suggest for further understanding that one read Lonergan's *Grace and Freedom* and his discussion of this issue in *Insight*. For those who are not metaphysically inclined, I would simply suggest viewing God as the Holy Mystery and adoring this Mystery. I should stress, however, that this argument is absolutely crucial to the differentiation between process philosophy and classical Thomistic philosophy in their radical difference regarding the divine unchangeableness. Is God simple or complex? Does God in God's self-experience feelings of compassion, and the like, or does God's desire to be one with us in suffering underlie his reason for becoming truly man in Jesus Christ with all that this implies, while at the same time remaining God. In the incarnation there is one divine Person, the eternal Word, who takes on a human nature while at the same time retaining his divine nature. This is why, as I have said before, the Council of Ephesus declared Mary to be truly the Mother of God in the Word made flesh.

Chapter Twenty-Three

The Origin of the Cosmos

John Navone

Our need for meaning primordially expresses itself in the narrative mode. Storytelling satisfies this need and desire by intending an intelligible, coherent, meaningful world. Our myths and stories of God, a constant in human history, witness to our spontaneous conviction that order prevails over chaos, that reality is intelligible. They imply our will to believe that the world is ultimately intelligible and that the absurd is not the last word.

Our desires for meaning and for knowledge strive to join our narrative expression with our will to believe. They give rise to the stories that provide the context for belief in God. The dynamics of our desire to know uncover a meaning that anticipates some form of narrative expression. This occurs even through our desire to know leads through apparent meaninglessness. The desire of both the desire to know and the will to believe in God merge in their intention of an intelligible world. The meaningfulness of such a world is experienced, lived and felt within some narrative framework; for life without story would be experienced as absurd.

Story links our feelings with the reality of ourselves. Story is the integrating structure that organizes our feelings and forms a sense of continuous identity with our past and future. Story brings a temporal context of meaning to the immediacy of the moment; otherwise, we would be forever losing our grip on the reality of our own identity with the passage of discrete moments. Mental balance involves keeping in touch with the narrative sequence underlying our thought. The impulse to tell or retell stories gives the lie to the claims that the world is absurd; for it is a way of ordering the world, which implies that the world is intelligible. The dynamics of narrative consciousness in storytelling intend a coherent universe and disclose our world-ordering impulse and power.

A spontaneous narrative consciousness persists and functions on the premise that there is a permanent meaning at the heart of things. Its resurgent tendency to shape the world with myth and story, despite every obstacle, implicitly affirms that the universe is not absurd. Ordering the coherence of the universe is not futile; it testifies to a primal conviction that reality lays itself open to being ordered in a comprehensible way, and that this would not take place if there were a primal conviction that the reality is absurd. The spontaneous world-ordering acts of storytelling involve a primal consciousness that is so intimately one with its world that it has not yet made the theoretical distinction between the human subject and its world. Such spontaneous primal thinking does not need to question whether the universe in itself is intelligibly ordered, for ordering (subject) and recognizing the world as already ordered (object) become different only to theoretical judgment. The spontaneous narrative consciousness involves an order that is also the order of the totality embracing both subject and object.

Narrative activity intending a meaningful world is the ontological ground for affirming that we are empowered to create such a world. Human vitality takes the form of intentionality; it is given to creating meaning and to affirming its own identity. Animal vitality, on the other hand, simply acts according to inalterable biological routines. Narrative consciousness is ultimately rooted in the ontological power of being or Being-Itself (God). Our participation in this power grounds our ineluctable need to order the world through stories. The dynamic of narrative consciousness postulates the supremacy of an intelligible universe over an indifferent one, of meaning over absurdity, of being over nonbeing. The persistent workings of our narrative consciousness postulate our participation in the power of meaningful being over and against the void, the possibility of new meaning revising our sense of reality and relating us in new ways to the world. Our will to believe in an intelligible world activates our narrative consciousness and the worlds of meaning that it opens up to us. Reflection on our narrative consciousness becomes that basis for our awareness of our desire to know and the postulate of a rational universe, a world-to-be-known in a questioning and critical way. Our narrative consciousness (the dynamic of storytelling) posits that there is intelligibility to be grasped in the world; otherwise we would not have sought it out. There would be no storytelling without the anticipation or foreknowledge, however vague, of some story to be told. And we would not continually revise our stories (and histories) if we did not anticipate some further intelligibility. Storytelling is undertaken on the premise that the real is comprehensible, meaningful, and intelligible. (Even our question about the intelligibility of the real posits intelligibility as the horizon of our questioning).

Chapter Twenty-Four

Laws and Structures

Bernard Tyrrell

It is possible to view evolution either from a scientific viewpoint or from a philosophical/theological viewpoint. Of course, concretely, they belong together, but each with its distinctive goals and methods. One error, which has caused a good number of problems recently, is to think that the sciences; for example, physics, chemistry, biology, can prove the existence of God utilizing their own methodology. In fact, each of the sciences has its own scope and limitations and the sciences I just mentioned are limited to proposing hypotheses that in principle need to be empirically tested and are subject to the principle of falsifiability.

Daniel Dennett has written a very lengthy work entitled *Darwin's Dangerous Idea*. But, is Darwin's discovery of the evolutionary nature of the cosmos dangerous and if so, to whom or to what? Evolution—stripped of its materialist, reductionist characteristics—is a theory that today enjoys wide acceptance in scientific communities and in Christian communities, including the Catholic community. But, it is rejected by some Christian communities. Lonergan has proposed a model of evolution that he calls emergent probability. It is complex, but I will try to articulate the gist of it here.

Lonergan distinguishes between classical and statistical laws. Classical law ignores concrete occurrences—all other things being equal—whereas statistical law deals with the detail of concrete happenings. A classical law would be that water freezes at 32 degrees Fahrenheit. A statistical law would indicate how often in a particular area the temperature gets down to freezing. These two laws together reveal that the universe is not bound by iron clad necessity. Change, genetic development, and even miracles are possible.

The Big Bang occurred approximately 12 billion years ago. Emergent probability initially supposes the spatial distribution of unimaginably large amounts of inanimate matter over amazing lengthy intervals of time. The number of particles, galaxies, stars that formed is almost incalculable. The length of time and space involved eventually allows in sequence the possibility, probability, and then actuality of schemes of recurrence. A rather simple example of a scheme of occurrence would be the way we develop a habit. We have to engage in a series of activities even to learn how to tie our shoelaces. Once we develop a habit new possibilities open up. Technically, then, for Bernard Lonergan, a scheme of recurrence is expressed by the formula, if A, then B, if B then C, then the reoccurrence of A. When A reoccurs you now have a pattern that has developed and it opens up the probability of new, more complex schemes occurring. Lonergan, unlike Darwin, spoke of schemes of occurrence rather than the emergence of individual things. The latter do not emerge independently, but within a cyclic arrangement that depends on an ambient occurring of events and other factors. Lonergan is concerned with probabilities of emergence and of survival.

The existence of schemes of recurrence occurs on the level of physics as particles interact with one another in a patterned series of events and this pattern in turn leads to the possibility and even probability of the emergence of more complex schemes. On the higher level of chemistry, which depends on the existence of the lower levels of ever more complex schemes on the level of physics, there arises the possibility, probability, and then actuality of schemes of occurrence constitutive of the chemical level. An example might be the occurrence of molecular schemes of recurrence, which in turn give rise to more complex schemes of recurrence. Eventually, there is the emergence of biology, which presupposes the complex schemes of physics and chemistry but goes beyond them with its own schemes of recurrence. An example of such a scheme might be the occurrence of plant eating animals before the occurrence of meat eating animals. It is only the existence of plant eating animals that makes meat eating animals realistically possible. As these schemes keep occurring and reoccurring the probability increases that a higher reality with its own possible, probable, and actual schemes of occurrence and recurrence comes to be. But, we should keep in mind that besides the probability of schemes of occurrence developing there is also the probability of the survival of schemes that must be taken into account. The human being eventually emerges with a spiritual soul created by God and in the human being evolution becomes conscious of itself. All the other levels of physics, chemistry, and biology are maintained, but transcended in the occurrence of the human being. At this point, we see how the human being now plays a crucial role as far as the survival both of itself and of certain lower schemes of occurrence and recurrence. An all-out use of a certain number of the approximately twenty three thousand nuclear weapons in existence could possibly eliminate not only human beings, but also animals and plant life.

Chapter Twenty-Four

Laws and Structures

John Navone

The affirmation that God speaks in history presupposes a basic metaphysics. To speak or not to speak is ultimately a question for metaphysics.

Metaphysics is neither some vague view of life nor some subtle intuition of Being. It is not a general account of reality, nor a process of linguistic clarification. Metaphysics is a structured anticipation of what is to be known, and the basic component in that structure is human wonder about human experience.

This wonder is expressed in two complementary types of question: a what-question or a why-question, and in another mode whose satisfaction is expressed in a simple Yes or No.

Our structured wonder is often unformulated or thematized as it was by Aristotle; nevertheless, it is an invariant structure that grounds metaphysics. This invariant structure is shared by all humankind, always and everywhere. It is a dynamic structure that pushes for reasons (why?) and for truth (is it so?).

The dynamic structure of human knowing involves many distinct activities of which none by itself may be named human knowing. It is the total combination of experience, understanding, and judgment, which assembles itself consciously, intelligently, and rationally. One part summons forth the next until the whole is reached: experience stimulates inquiry, and inquiry leads from experience through imagination to insight, and from insight to concepts, which stimulate reflection (the conscious exigence of rationality). Reflection marshals the evidence to judge Yes or No, or else to doubt and so renew inquiry.

We are a part of history. Because of our structured dynamism of wonder, we inevitably question our historical experience and are also questioned by it. The objective, dynamic world-order of which we are a part raises questions for our understanding. The human dynamism of inquiry is an integral part of the developing world-order, of the interlocking, created, temporal universe which is history.

How does God "speak" in history? Departing from the material aspect for the meaning and truth of the expression "Word of God," we can understand the prophetic dictum, "The word of the Lord came to me," as an interpretation of history in which the proper judgmental element is supplied by prophetic light and the formal element by the ideas conceived in a human way by the prophet or writer.

God uses the things of the universe to convey his mind, as we use the written and spoken word to convey ours. For Aquinas, the movement of a pen or vocal cord is not less subject to our dominion than the course of events is subject to divine providence. The intelligibility of things derives from what they are, and from the Mind that employs them to express Itself.

Generalizing this Thomistic principle, we may say that the totality of history is God's Word. Nor is history, the totality of the created, developing, world-order, an inferior means of communication, as if words openly stated the mind of the speaker, whereas one could only infer from events the mind of God. Words are just black marks on paper or vibrations in the air apart from the intelligence of the speaker or receiver. In themselves, they are just data, potentially intelligible, on the immediate level. The totality of history is a divine creation, no more unwieldy an instrument of meaning than the human artifact of language.

Both truth and meaning are, strictly speaking, in the minds of persons and in their minds only. Words in an unknown language, whether written or spoken, have no meaning for us. The lack is not on the page, in the transmitted vibrations, but in ourselves. We are the basic source of meaning for the document, the vibrations, the events, and the greater our understanding of the language and of the subject written or spoken about, the more meaning they have for us. This does not imply meaning is subjective; rather, the ink-marks on paper, the vibrations, the events, all are only signs of meaning and not the meaning of truth itself.

The marks, vibrations, and events can be signs of meaning, and there can be a correct meaning, which comes only through long efforts at understanding. Over a period of time the documents, words, or events, might have meant something different to each successive generation; however, the meaning need not be opposed. The first understanding might have been correct, but inadequate; and basically what was developing was not certainty but understanding. By the same token, our understanding of documents, and of the dynamic world-order of the created universe (of God's Word, history) can develop.

Chapter Twenty-Five

Evolution and Creationism

Bernard Tyrrell

We have only presented schematic elements of Lonergan's theory of emergent probability. To present it in all its details would require a book in itself. Now we need to look at the philosophical/theological foundations of the theory of emergent probability. In this chapter, I rely very heavily on Lonergan's Mission and Spirit article in *A Third Collection*. Lonergan distinguishes three types of finality. These are the absolute, the horizontal, and the vertical.

Absolute finality is to God since every finite, limited instance of the good has both its goal and ground in absolute goodness. Horizontal finality is to the proportionate end, this results from what a thing is, what it does and may do. Vertical finality is to an end higher than the proportionate end and it presupposes a hierarchy of entities and ends and a subordination of the lower to the higher. This subordination is at times instrumental and at times participative. Sometimes it may be both. As instrumental it serves the higher, but as participative it enters into the being and functioning of the higher. For example, as participative, subatomic particles some way enter into the elements of the periodic table of chemistry; chemical elements enter into chemical compounds and these in turn enter into cells and these in diverse ways enter into the biological constitution of plants and then animals.

What is most important to keep in mind, is that in an authentic evolutionary view all of these developments can only be adequately accounted for by bringing in the cause of the entire universe. This is so because it is only through the cause of the universe that the lower as lower, acting beyond its natural proportion, is able to bring about participation in the higher. Only the ultimate cause is able to bring forth the movement from lower species to successively higher species. Biology is then deficient to the extent that it can only observe the evolutionary process within the limits of its own methodology and this necessarily excludes the possibility that biology itself can provide ultimate answers to questions that naturally arise in reflecting on biology, but which are beyond the methodological limits of biology.

Lonergan bestows high praise on Darwin for his breakthrough in grasping that evolution does occur. But, he sharply rejects certain materialistic and deterministic theories of evolution. Lonergan speaks of probabilities of emergence instead of Darwin's natural selection and he speaks of probabilities of survival where Darwin speaks of the survival of the fittest. There are many nuances involved in Lonergan's theory of emergent probability. But, the bottom line is that the omniscient and omnipotent cause of the whole universe does not operate blindly. Rather God plans where scientists turn to probabilities. And nothing occurs or comes into existence outside of God's plan nor can any agent interfere with God's design.

Recently, there have been various proposals of Intelligent Design as proving the existence of a Designer. I have no problem with Intelligent Design if we are speaking philosophically of God as the efficient, exemplary, and final cause of the universe. As exemplary cause, God is the cause of the existence of any pattern or design that occurs in the universe. But, it is necessary to observe that the physicist as physicist, the chemist as chemist, the biologist as biologist cannot use the occurrence of certain complex designs they discover in their respective sciences to attempt to prove the existence of the Ultimate Designer or God. The scope and limitations of their own empirical methods do not allow this. This is why the creationists and others cannot demand that the proving of the existence of an Intelligent Designer be made part of the subject matter of courses such as those of physics, chemistry, and biology. It is up to the philosophers and theologians to reflect on the issues of the existence of God and God's attributes through the use of deficient analogies based on existing created realities. One atheist recently stated that "philosophy is dead." It is only a "cover up" for knowledge the hard sciences have not yet discovered. But, and here is the rub, the statement that philosophy is dead is itself a philosophical statement since the methods of the hard sciences cannot empirically prove or disprove this statement.

Chapter Twenty-Five

Evolution and Creationism

John Navone

God reveals himself as the ultimate source of revelation in all its phases. His primary revelation for us is the visible world He created and through which He speaks. The totality of history is God's Word; the one universe with its natural and supernatural components, the *magnalia Dei* in history and the operations of human beings; the entire dynamic of the world-order from beginning to end with its sacred and secular aspects.

For the community of Christian faith, the form, or structure, of human history has already been given in Christ, its permanent meaning through all material changes. The Father sends the Son, whose Incarnation assumes the material universe of time and space (history) into the Trinitarian life. The Father and the Son send the Spirit for the definitive work of sanctification. The three Persons come to inhabit the souls of the just. The events of history, the material element of this phase of revelation, will be completed at the end of time when the number of the just has been completed.

On the subjective side, there is the inner light needed to interpret the objective and the historical. This light is necessary because the supernatural component of history is beyond the penetration of native human intelligence and judgment on the subjective side.

In *Offenbarung als Geschichte*, W. Pannenberg affirms that the idea of the supernatural should be excluded because everything that happens in history is the expression of the working of the one triune God. He affirms that God's self-revelation through his deeds is open for everyone to see in "ordinary history." There is no need of faith or supernatural aid to recognize this. Ultimately, it takes the whole of history to manifest God.

The whole of history cannot adequately manifest God. Only proper knowledge of God can fully meet the question of what God is. Reception in the intellect of an intelligible form proportionate to the object that is understood is necessary for proper knowledge. This knowledge is an act of understanding in virtue of a form proportionate to the object; hence, proper knowledge of God must be in virtue of an infinite form, in virtue of God himself. Such knowledge surpasses the natural proportion of any possible, created, finite substance and so is strictly supernatural.

Whatever knowledge history mediates of God will be analogous. The sacred is always beyond whatever knowledge we have of it. Analogous knowledge provides the intellect with some lesser form that bears some resemblance to the object to be understood and thereby yields some understanding of it. Because history that mediates our knowledge of God differs from the object to be understood, which is God himself, it must be complemented by the corrections of the *via affirmationis, negationis, et eminentiae* as in natural theology.

All spheres of the profane mediate the sacred; the character of the mediated knowledge is analogous. Knowledge of God, mediated through history, does not and cannot fully satisfy the human intellect. Such knowledge answers some questions and raises others. Because it is analogous knowledge, the more we learn about God through the mediation of history, the clearer it becomes that there is much we do not know.

The meaning of history is measured by the infinite mind of God and unrestricted by human conceptions. Because the meaning of the divine word cannot be exhausted, the meaning in revelation will never be exhausted. God alone knows the meaning of history. Paul spoke a word which is his and God's; however, the meaning is limited by the meaning that Paul gave it. History, as the totality of creation with its natural and supernatural components, is the Word that God alone speaks in much the same way that we move pen and vocal cords in revealing ourselves.

We live and move and have our being within the Word, history, which God speaks. Our spirit is marked by its questioning character and almost constituted by inquiry. Our understanding of God will be mediated by the Word, by the totality of history, in which our existence is rooted. It will be mediated by the dynamic world-order; consequently, our performance in questioning history implicitly manifests our dialogue with God, who speaks it. Implicit in every human inquiry is a natural desire to know God by his essence; implicit in every human judgment about contingent things is the formally unconditioned/without limitation that is God; implicit in every human choice of values is the absolute good that is God. We are a component of the word and question it. In the dynamic of the question, God speaks as the Question-Raising and Question-Answering Mystery in human history, even if implicitly and anonymously.

Chapter Twenty-Six

Bias, Meaning, and Meaninglessness
Bernard Tyrrell

We now turn from the discussion of evolution in nature to the developments or evolutions that have taken place in the 2,000 year history of the Catholic Church and in part in other more recent Christian churches. The Church is an institution embedded deeply in history. All members of the Catholic Church are sinners, as are all human beings. This Church has been around for over two thousand years and so it is burdened with the reality that many individuals and groups in its history have done evil things. This includes popes and paupers, the well-known and the long forgotten. How can one critique the Catholic Church in an authentic way; how can one avoid bias of some kind? Here I am using the term bias in a pejorative manner.

Aristotle begins his magisterial *Metaphysics* by remarking that all men are endowed with a desire to know. Aristotle was a realist; he maintained that we really can come to true knowledge about ourselves and the universe in varying degrees. Two forms of bias are individual bias and group bias. An example of individual bias is when a person inevitably attributes evil motivation to whatever another person says or does. Group bias occurs when a social group of individuals, such as the supporters of slavery, blinds itself to any evidence contrary to their view. The natural desire to know, which Aristotle speaks of, can be blocked in its functioning by bias. Both atheists and Christians can be subject to these forms of bias and this is true of others as well.

When one of the contemporary atheists states that "religion poisons everything" he is blinded by bias. No one can reasonably deny that the Catholic and other Christian churches have contributed much to the positive aspects of Western Civilization, from monks translating manuscripts to groups of religious women founding hospitals. At the same time, Catholics must acknowledge that much evil has been done by individuals and groups in the two thousand years of church history, from the inquisitions to the unenlightened undermining of Native American cultures in the name of Christ.

How then can a person or groups of individuals reduce their biases to a minimum? Moral, spiritual, and intellectual conversions are the pathway to authenticity in one's knowing, willing, and acting. Moral conversion involves doing the right thing in the right way even when it goes against certain selfish desires and proclivities. This is what Aristotle defines as the truly virtuous person.

Spiritual conversion means openness to the many dimensions of human experience and not the automatic exclusion of any consideration of the possibility of a transcendence that goes beyond the merely material. The same, of course, can also be said of those who a priori deny the reality of the material elements of the universe, which is the case in some philosophies and religions, such as certain Eastern philosophies and a religion like Christian Science (this is not to imply that a Christian Scientist may not be an authentically good and holy individual). Spiritual conversion is at its deepest level surrender to a personal, transcendent God. But, the atheist who sincerely seeks to be faithful to the authentic inner summons of his or her mind and heart may actually have God's own love poured into his or her heart, but is not able to give a name to this inner experience. Inversely, a so called believer can espouse a belief system without authentically surrendering his or her mind and heart in thought and action to God. Karl Rahner famously said that a person may be an atheist in the head, but a theist in the heart and vice versa.

Intellectual conversion in its simplest form is ongoing fidelity to the call to be attentive, understanding, reasonable, and responsible in his or her thoughts, words, and actions. Intellectual conversion in its more technical meaning is seeking an answer to three questions: What am I doing when I am knowing, why is doing that knowing, and what do I know when I do it? But, this form of intellectual conversion is not required of everyone who seeks to live authentically. Rather it only occurs by engaging in a philosophical quest to reach a personally validated answer to these three philosophical questions.

Chapter Twenty-Six

Bias, Meaning, and Meaninglessness
John Navone

History, the Word that God speaks, triggers the human dynamics of the question. It raises questions and stimulates inquiry. It constitutes our precarious situation with the possibility of failure or of fuller development. The Word, which God speaks to us and which "contains" him, offers possibilities of human development in the dynamism constituting human consciousness that may be expressed by the imperatives: be attentive, be intelligent, be reasonable, and be responsible. The imperatives regard every human inquiry, judgment, decision, and choice.

Any failure to be human implies an abdication from history. Our dynamism for inquiry is a part of history which makes us responsible to history as God's Word. As a part of God's historical word, we transcend ourselves in answering that word through the intelligence of our inquiry, the reasonableness of our judgments, the responsibility of our decisions and choices. The absence of intelligence, of reason, of responsibility in our inquiry, judgment, decision, and choice, distances us from history, from the meaning with which God actually constitutes history as his temporal self-expression.

History *is* ultimately what it means to God who freely speaks it. In this respect, history *is* what it *means* and history *means* what it is. Meaning constitutes history. Meaning and existence are convertible. God is uncreated meaning creating meaning; God is Eternal Meaning creating historical meaning. All spheres of the profane mediate the sacred; all spheres of historical meaning mediate the meaning of the supra-historical from which it derives. Limited meaning bespeaks infinite meaning; historical meaning bespeaks eternal meaning. In this way, history is God's limited, temporal self-expression: it is the limited, temporal expression of his meaning. Meaning is God's "speaking" in history; rather, God "speaks" history as Eternal Meaning expressing Itself in temporal meaning.

In virtue of our existence, we participate in history; in virtue of our meaning, we express God's historical self-revelation. Only the meaningful is desirable (lovable); therefore, only the lovable mediates God's self-revelation. The pure desire to know the meaningful is an intrinsic component of our make-up, even if it does not consistently and completely dominate our consciousness. It is our openness to history as fact and decision, for love is the proper emanation of desire. The achievement, which is always implied in our openness to history, is a question of the pure, unrestricted desire's full functioning, of its dominating consciousness through precepts, methods, criticism, a formulated view of knowledge, and of the reality of our knowledge can attain.

Divine grace brings openness as gift, when our pure desire to know the meaningful is no longer restricted to the limited and the historical, even though it conditions it and is conditioned by it. Openness as fact (the self as ground of all higher aspiration) and openness as achievement (self-appropriation) which arises from the fact, are an openness to history, to created meaning extending from the beginning to the end of time, the finite expression of uncreated Meaning.

The possibility of openness defined by the pure desire for meaning is intended for openness as gift, which implies the enlargement of a horizon that is not naturally possible for humankind, because such an enlargement is beyond the resources of finite consciousness. Openness as gift involves the transformation of the subject when it is aware of itself as the gift of self by God to self. It is awareness of personal relations with God. It is the actual openness of the natural desire to the ultimate Meaning of history, mediated by the temporal, limited meaning of history.

We are made for meaning. Our pure, unrestricted desire for meaning enables us to inquire into everything about everything. It implies a desire for unlimited participation in history, in created meaning, through successive enlargements of our actual horizon.

The enlargement of horizon following upon grace conditions our interpretation of history, of created meaning, which we interpret according to a faith principle. History has a new meaning that results from "adding" the supernatural; however, the condition is not mathematical. It is the intimate and complete transformation of all the historical, of the human, so as to give it, not a new material reality, but a new meaning. Christian marriage, for example, may differ little in appearances from non-Christian marriage; however, it is different, because its meaning is different: it has the meaning of the union of Christ and his church (Eph 5).

Chapter Twenty-Seven

Beliefs, History, and Metaphysics

Bernard Tyrrell

Basically, most of what we say we know we actually believe. We define belief as accepting as true something based on the testimony of another. Thus, I have never personally met President Obama, but in relying on the testimony of the media and other sources I believe that he exists, although I have never personally verified that he does exist. Religious beliefs, like all other beliefs, are based on the testimony of others whom we trust for the veracity of these beliefs. I must immediately add that not all religious beliefs are true and that to distinguish true religious beliefs from those that are false we must look very carefully at the credibility of those on whose trustworthiness we rely. Contemporary atheists, however, will not accept any religious belief that cannot be empirically tested according to the rigorous methodology of empiricism.

As we have seen earlier, Catholic and some other Christian believers trust in the reliability of the testimony of the earliest Christians, the sacred writings approved by these early Christians, the faithfulness of those who followed after them and the sacred traditions they promoted and fully embraced. Of course, they above all relied on God and the divine gift of the inner light of faith that enabled them to firmly believe in the Good News in all its dimensions.

If we seek evidence that the present Catholic faith is in continuity with the earliest Christian beliefs one of the most striking examples is found in the Letters of Ignatius of Antioch that he wrote to bishops on his way to Rome to be martyred. There is basic agreement that he wrote these brief letters around 110 A.D. This was about the same time as the writings attributed to John the apostle were completed. What is most striking about these brief, beautiful letters of Ignatius (we urge you to read them) is the stress on bishops' authority, the recognition of the divinity of Christ, the Eucharist as Catholic's understand it today and a variety of other beliefs and practices still accepted today. Ignatius was clearly aware of the apostolic tradition and may have known John the apostle or at least individuals who personally knew some of the apostles. Polycarp who wrote not so many years after Ignatius and was also martyred knew Ignatius and acknowledged his legitimacy. Polycarp (69-125 A.D.) was martyred at the age of 83. Next we have Irenaeus (140-202), a hearer of Polycarp. Irenaeus was the first to recognize the truly inspired character of the four Gospels as we know them. It is very important to note that oral tradition preceded the actual writing of the epistles and Gospels and that it was the authorities in the early church who decided which scriptures were authentic and which were not. Irenaeus also wrote that the only way for Christians to retain unity was to accept one doctrinal authority, namely Episcopal councils in union with the bishop of Rome.

Chapter Twenty-Seven

Beliefs, History, and Metaphysics

John Navone

J ohn Haldane explains why Stephen Hawking's attempt to banish natural theology only shows why we need it ("Philosophy Lives" *First Things*, Jan. 2011, 43-46). Haldane affirms that Stephen Hawking and Leonard Mlodinow, in their book *The Grand Design*, claim that philosophy is dead because it has not kept pace with modern developments in science, particularly physics. Scientists, for them, have become the bearers of the torch of discovery in our quest for knowledge. They claim that both philosophy and natural theology have passed away because the traditional argument from the order apparent in the structure and operations of the universe to a transcendent cause of these, namely God, is wholly redundant. The apparently miraculous design of living forms can appear without the intervention of a supreme being, a benevolent creator, who made the universe for our benefit. Spontaneous creation is the reason there is something rather than nothing, why the universe exists, why we exist.

Although the universe could have been spatially and temporally chaotic, Haldane affirms that it isn't. We know that the observable universe is composed of a number of types of entities and forces whose members exhibit common properties and are subject to a small number of simple laws. From chemistry, we learn that elements share well-defined structural properties in virtue of which they can and do enter into systematic combination; from physics we learn that these elements are themselves constructed out of more basic items whose properties are ever purer and simpler.

Why is there order rather than chaos? If there had been chaos, the question would not arise because we would not exist. Cosmic regularity makes our existence possible. The underlying issue concerns the enabling conditions of this order itself. Some reason that, while events in nature can be explained by reference to the fundamental particles and the laws under which they operate, natural science cannot explain these factors. Natural explanations having reached their logical limit, we must conclude that either the orderliness of the universe has no explanation or that it has an extra-natural one. Haldane believes that the search for the source of order must reach a dead end if scientific explanation is the only sort there is. It is not, however, the only sort; there is also explanation by reference to purpose and intention.

The universe's otherwise inexplicable regularity will have an adequate explanation if it derives from the purposes of an agent. Inasmuch as no natural agent could have made the universe, Haldane concludes that the only possible explanation of its regularity is that the natural order has a transcendent cause outside of the universe, which introduces the idea of a creator God.

Aquinas and others in the Western natural-theology tradition argued from the character of the universe to the existence of its transcendent cause. They were acute enough to describe that original source of the being and character of things as an uncaused cause and not as the cause of itself. That was a matter of logical coherence, since the idea that something could create itself from nothing itself makes no sense, be that something God or the universe. In order to create, one first has to exist.

The basic components of the material universe and the forces operating on them exhibit properties of stability and regularity that invite explanation. Science cannot provide an ultimate explanation of order.

Chapter Twenty-Eight

Creator, Creation, and Revelation
Bernard Tyrrell

God is not a "God of the gaps." This is the atheist phrase for the God that theists affirm to be the ultimate explanation for everything beyond their comprehension: the Reality that ultimately fills in all the gaps in their understanding. God is the creator of the universe out of nothing. God is the conserver in being of everything that exists and without this ongoing conserving action of God everything finite that now exists would cease to be. God is the first agent of every event, every development, and every emergent. God makes use of secondary causes (created causes) as instruments in executing the divine plan for the order of the universe. God is at work in every aspect of creation because God is the ultimate cause of everything. God understands every possible universe in all its details, including free choices made in these diverse possible worlds. God does not put the universe together part by part, but as a complete whole. There are those who view the present universe as the best universe God could create. This may be correct, although Thomas Aquinas held the opposite position. There are also those who hold that God would have become incarnate in the present universe even if no original sin had occurred. This was the view of some Franciscans and others. This may be correct, although Aquinas disagreed with this view.

Lonergan agrees with Aquinas who in one of his most mature commentaries on Aristotle takes the view that God possesses a transcendent causality that is unique to God alone and is beyond creaturely cause/effect relationships. Through God's transcendent causality God is able to create free acts of rational beings without in any way interfering with the freedom of the creature in making these free choices. As we have seen earlier, Lonergan offers an explanation of how this is logically possible without involving a contradiction or the negation of truly human free choices; but, I do not think that it is necessary for our limited purposes here to present in yet more detail Lonergan's lengthy argument. One who is interested in this particular argument can find it in his works *Grace and Freedom* and *Insight*.

Revelation, as we have seen, occurs within a historical context. There is a gradual unfolding of revelation. Early on the Jewish people believed that Yahweh was supreme among gods. Gradually a strict monotheism developed under the guidance of the Spirit. At certain times, development was dynamic and at other times static. There is an operator and an integrator at work in individual human beings and in cultural periods as well. Without the operator there would not be any development in individuals or in cultures as a whole. At the same time without the integrator there would be no maintenance of habits (we don't have to relearn every morning how to tie and untie our shoelaces); at the same time without the operator we would never be able to break old habits or to develop new habits. In historical and sacred historical developments, there needs to be both a progressive and conservative principle at work. Archeological and sacred historical periods reveal times in which development occurred rather rapidly and other times which were relatively static and stable.

Most felicitously Jewish and Christian revelations undergo developments involving understanding deeper meanings present in God's Word in history. The abolition of slavery in America (it is still going forward to a certain extent) and the recognition of women's right to vote did not happen overnight. Some religions are more open to developments than others, but all are subject to the vagaries of history. At the turn of the nineteenth and early in the twentieth century the church was in a conservative period with its focus on Modernism; but once again Vatican II seemed to come out of nowhere in a relatively brief period of time imbued with a progressive motion. Today, we are still struggling to reach a balance between the old and the new. Questions have been raised which neither secular society nor the Christian churches have yet to find fully satisfying answers. But, we have the promise of Jesus that his Spirit will always be with us and so we remain blessed with faith-filled hope.

Chapter Twenty-Eight

Creator, Creation, and Revelation

John Navone

Creation, according to Thomas Aquinas, is the primary and most perfect revelation of the Divine; therefore, if we do not understand creation correctly, we cannot hope to understand God correctly.

St. Bonaventure and Blessed John Duns Scotus held that the whole of creation was the necessary preparation for the divine Incarnation in Jesus, the Human One. The fleshing of God was not a later rescue attempt to put the original, failed plan back on track. Fall or no fall, it was lovingly willed from the very beginning.

Two thousand years ago, the human Incarnation of God in Jesus happened, but before that, in the original incarnation of the amazing story of evolution, God had already begun the mysterious process of becoming flesh by participating in creation itself. In this respect, the Incarnation of God did not only happen in Bethlehem, 2,000 years ago. It actually began 14 billion years ago with a moment we call The Big Bang.

Cosmologist and cultural historian Thomas Berry points out that Jesus did not come into a world, added on later, so to speak, as a necessary afterthought; He came into a world that was made originally in and through himself as the creative context of existence. Berry identifies the Christ story with the story of the universe, the revelation of the Logos and Love that is the origin, ground, and destiny of creation. The Christ story expresses the holiness of creation itself.

Against any denigration of the material world, Christianity offers the vision of a beautiful, created world that can lead towards the spiritual, informing presence of the Word of God. But at the same time, the very goals of philosophy—awareness of the intelligible and purification of the soul—are taken up and rendered universally possible through our faith in God's redemptive drawing us towards eternal life. In this perspective, Christianity can be shown to be not only a religion that is at odds with pagan religious practices, but a way of life that surpasses that idealized by the Greek philosopher Plato who viewed the material temporal world as the cause of unhappiness, and hence emphasizing the need for us to remove ourselves from absorption with the world and contemplate ever more deeply eternal verities and archetypes.

The Christian liturgy resists Platonism's aversion to the material temporal world through its vision of a liturgy in which the one Creator of all acts in the community, drawing the world to its consummation: Christian worship draws the hearts and minds of the faithful to Christ and through Christ to the one Father of all. In the sacramental mode of its liturgy, the world acknowledges and celebrates its very being as flowing from the Eternal Now of God, and in each passing moment moving inevitably towards its divine fulfillment in both the Love that sustains the cosmos and in the Logos that is its meaning.

The liturgy is a primary source for Christian thought about God, creation, redemption and related doctrines. This was a feature of early church theology, summed up in the phrase *lex orandi lex est credendi*: the rule of praying governs or constitutes the form and content of believing. The liturgy both forms and expresses human beings in the Christian faith, in any given age or tradition. The deep structures of what it means to remember, to praise, to bless, to give thanks, to invoke, to offer sacrifice and to supplicate are at the heart of Christian worship and its cosmic relevance.

Chapter Twenty-Nine

Hell

Bernard Tyrrell

The militant atheists find the idea of hell an abomination. How can God punish individuals with an eternity of torment? Catholic Christian belief does affirm the reality of the states of purgatory, heaven, and hell. One cannot ignore these doctrines except at one's peril. The doctrine of purgatory makes sense on the common sense level. Actions have consequences and many of us die not completely loving God with all our heart, soul, mind, and strength and all others. Purgatory is the Catholic way of dealing with what Buddhists call "bad karma." However, unlike Buddhists the solution for Catholics is not reincarnation, but a "one time" cleansing of the soul so that it can enter forever into the Divine Presence pure and free of all remnants of sin and its effects.

Jean Paul Sartre in his play *No Exit* ends with the line "Hell is other people." Sartre unknowingly is describing the actual state of people subject to damnation. In the final analysis Christianity may be summed up in the statement: God loves us unconditionally and it is our calling during our pilgrimage here on earth to love God with all our heart and soul and mind and strength and to love all others as God has loved and will always love us. Love is the way to heaven and the lack of love both of God and of neighbor is the pathway to hell. John of the Cross writes that at the end of life we will be judged by Love. If we fail lastingly and permanently to love God and our neighbor then we die in a state of lovelessness. It is not that God ceases to love us at any time, but instead of loving and enjoying God and all the saints those in hell will exist in a self-imposed state of alienation or indifference toward God and all the saints. In this state "Hell is [indeed] other people [and God.]" But, after this grim assessment, we need to look at the doctrine of hope and to recall the intriguing statement of Julian of Norwich that "in the end all will be well and all manner of things will be well."

The theologian Hans Urs von Balthasar entitles one of his many books *Dare We Hope that All may be Saved?* If I read him correctly he answers this question in the affirmative. Do I hope more for my own salvation than for the salvation of others? Jesus tells us not to judge others lest we ourselves be judged. One hopes not just for oneself, but for others as well. There is always the possibility of a death bed moment of conversion. Some speak of a final option in which we choose or do not choose God on the basis of how we have lived. Inasmuch as Jesus teaches that all things are possible with God, there is hope for the salvation of anyone and everyone. The Church has a canonization process that culminates in declaring that a certain person is a saint in heaven. On the contrary, the Church does not have a damnation process in which she declares that a particular individual is in hell. The parables of Jesus are filled with examples of mercy, as in the case of the Prodigal Son and the Good Shepherd seeking out the one lost sheep out of the 99 that are safe. In an inspired moment, John Paul II named the first Sunday after Easter as "Divine Mercy Sunday." We can always bank on the mercy of God as long as we are merciful to others.

Chapter Twenty-Nine

Hell

John Navone

Our image of hell is ultimately based on our image of God. Unfortunately, our false image of hell as a divine and eternal torture chamber reflects our false image of God that has helped to fuel the atheist movement's denial of the existence of such a monstrosity. False images of God ground our false image of hell. Only a true image of God can correct these false images and help to undo their evil impact within the Christian community of faith.

The popular image of hell as a divine and eternal torture center implies a blasphemous notion of an angry vengeful God who in no way squares with the Good News that God is Love and Thomas Aquinas's affirmation that God is Happiness Itself (*Summa Theologiae*, I-II, q.3, a.2)

There are many good reasons for rejecting the popular image of hell as a divine torture chamber. One of them is Aquinas' article in his *Summa Theologiae* affirming that God loves the devils in hell. They are not in hell because of a petulant and unloving God; rather, they are unable to enjoy God's love for them.

Creatures do not determine God's infinite love: our being good does not make God love us more; our being evil does not make God love us less. Our being in heaven or hell does not, respectively, increase or decrease God's love for us. Heaven is simply the state of our enjoying communion with God; hell is the state of our inability to enjoy God.

C.S. Lewis, in one of his novels, captures the notion of the difference between these two states when he describes his vision of persons walking barefooted across the grass of a sunlit meadow. Puzzled to see that some are radiantly smiling while others are painfully writhing, he asks one of the latter to explain how it is possible that there is such a difference in their reaction to the same walk through the sunlit meadow. The suffering stroller explains that the grass is reality, and it is dreadfully painful for their walking. The reality of God is what it is: Happiness Itself. Heaven is the state of those for whom God is a joy forever; hell is the state of those for whom God is not.

At the death of Jesus in Luke's Gospel, the crucified Jesus assures the good thief that today he shall be with him in paradise. To be in heaven, therefore, is essentially to be in communion with the crucified and risen Christ forever. To enjoy forever the true goodness and beauty of Happiness Itself, as Aquinas describes God, is to be in paradise/heaven. Hell, therefore, is the state of a missed opportunity to enjoy the gift of God's company. Hell is not the absence of God's love, but the absence of love for God.

Jesus tells parables about God's inviting us to the festivity of his banquet. The refusers of these festivities are persons who either have better and more important things to do or, like the elder brother of the Prodigal Son, who resent God's enjoyment of their "unworthy" siblings. Elder brothers who cannot understand their father's love for his children, even now, do not experience the happiness of Happiness Itself. Hell is the inability to share the joy of God in his creatures, in ourselves and all others.

Chapter Thirty

Is God Narcissistic in Asking for Our Worship?

Bernard Tyrrell

Why does God create us and require our absolute worship? The atheists claim that a God who requires worship from us is utterly self-centered. The idea of a heaven in which we worship God forever is for them the peak of the Jewish/Christian God's Absolute Narcissism. The Catholic view, on the contrary, is that God does not have to create. God in God's self is supreme Happiness and Joy Itself. Accordingly, God is free to create or not to create and gains nothing by creating us. What then is God's goal in creating? The First Vatican Council defined as a doctrine of the faith that God creates not to gain happiness for himself, but to share his happiness with us.

God asks us for worship then not for God's sake, but for our sake. God asks us for worship because it fulfills the deepest yearnings of our minds and hearts to do so. We are created in God's image and are drawn towards God in a certain sense like a magnet draws iron to itself. But, God draws us toward our authentic supernatural fulfillment without forcing us to respond positively. The greatest natural gift God gives us is freedom. The ability to respond freely to the gracious invitations God gives us is itself a gift, enabling us to enjoy the absolute Goodness and Beauty that God is.

Just as human lovers are free to respond to the beloved or not, so our free choice of God, always aided by God's grace, immeasurably enriches our communion with the Beloved. Jesus responds to his disciples questing with the question, "Why do you call me good? God alone is good" (Mk 10:13). Jesus is not here denying his own divinity and goodness but He is endeavoring to remind us that God alone is Goodness itself and the goal of all our seeking. Creaturely goodness pales in significance in comparison to the Absolute Goodness that God is. This is not to deny that as the moon is related to the light of the sun and shares in its brightness so too we possess true goodness and its richness, but only through the creative acts of God do we possess this goodness and apart from the divine Goodness that we mirror in a creaturely fashion we are nothing. God alone is the Absolute and so infinitely transcends all the goodness of the creature. This remains the case even when in heaven we see God, no longer through a glass darkly, but face to face. We will never cease to be graced creatures and this is why heaven will be dynamic and not static as we forever continuously discover new richness in the Holy Mystery that God is.

Chapter Thirty

Is God Narcissistic in Asking for Our Worship?

John Navone

If the old atheists maintained that belief in God is not true, the new atheists maintain that it is not good. John Blanchard notes ("Has Science Got Rid of God?" *Tabletalk Magazine*, Aug. 1, 2008, Reformed Theology Articles at Ligonier. org) that both old and new atheists make the following four claims.

Science explains why we are here. In this context, the word *why* can mean either how we got here or what is our purpose in being here. Dawkins affirms that *Homo sapiens* is the state-of-the-art product of a vast sequence of tightly related species and kinds, beginning with the first living cell and moving on through invertebrates, fish, amphibians, reptiles, birds, quadruped, and ape-like mammals.

If atheist evolutionists are right, we should expect to find our planet teeming with fossils of intermediate life forms—but they are not there.

Science explains the origin of life. In what he calls the central argument of *The God Delusion*, Dawkins claims that while so many things appear to have been designed, the impression is false because it raises the unanswerable question about who designed the designer. In response, we ask where is the scientific proof that the appearance of design is deceiving us? There is none. Secondly, science cannot prove that the designer must have been designed, in other words, that the Creator must have been created. In sum, is there any branch of science that can definitively rule out the possibility of a supernatural Creator?

As Ludwig Wittgenstein said in his monumental *Tractatus*: "The solution to the riddle of life in space and time lies outside space and time." This squares the biblical affirmation about God being "from everlasting to everlasting" (Ps 106:48) and its testimony that this transcendent and eternal Creator "gives life to all things" (1 Tim 6:13).

Science explains where the world came from. Although scientists have endless theories about the origin of the universe, science can never go any further back than the moment at which the laws on which it depends begin to operate. As Edgar Andrews, emeritus professor of materials at the University of London, notes "Science, even at its most speculative, must stop short of offering an explanation or even description of the actual event of origin."

Among the atheists who try to evade this issue is Peter Atkins, professor of chemistry at Oxford, who claims that the entire universe is an elaborate and engaging rearrangement of nothing in which space-time generates its own dust in the process of its own self-assembly.

Science explains what life is all about. That Dawkins makes such a claim is curious, inasmuch as he denies that human life has any purpose, describing such an idea as "a nearly universal delusion." He claims that human beings are merely "survival machines" blindly programmed to preserve the selfish molecules known as genes. He offers no explanation for the fact that as humans we are self-conscious, thinking beings, with an insatiable desire to know the truth of things, evaluate them, make choices and decisions. Nor does he explain our unique sense of dignity, personhood, commitments, loyalties, dreams, hopes, and aspirations. Dawkins fails to explain how an impersonal origin, plus time and chance, can give personhood.

Sir John Eccles, a Nobel Prize-winning pioneer in brain research, presses the point home in affirming that science cannot explain the existence of each of us as a unique self. Even Steve Jones, an ardent atheist and professor of genetics at University College, London, admits that science cannot answer the question why are we here.

Chapter Thirty-One

The Christian Experience and Its Critics
Bernard Tyrrell

There are major differences among peoples in belief and it is not possible here to look at all the diverse belief systems and whether they help or do not help individuals and societies to be spiritually, psychologically, and physically healthy. The new atheists generally would answer that religion is harmful, although there are differences among them about the degree and universality of harmfulness. Some, for example, stress that Buddhism is superior to the monotheistic religions because of its ambiguous or outright denial of the existence of the personal God of the three major monotheistic religions and the types of morality they embody. Yet, Christopher Hitchens and others, for example, have problems with Eastern religions as well as with the monotheistic religions. Here the focus will be on Christianity with special reference to Catholicism.

One can look at the Catholic faith from the Inside Out or from the Outside In. It makes all the difference in the world. When a couple is deeply in love and committed to one another for many years, with their varying ups and downs, their mutually entwined experiences of periods of pain and joy, of struggle and triumph, they have no need to critically validate the reality, richness and fruitfulness of their love for one another. The same can be said of authentic Christians and here specifically Catholic religious experience that is long and lasting. It is a multi-splendored reality. The core beliefs, the Biblical Word of God, the sacramental system with the Eucharist as its radiating core, the prayer (individual and communal, personal and liturgical), the testimony of repentant sinners and saints, the mystics and martyrs—all of these—are in themselves and above all taken together existentially self-validating as the richest dimension of the human experience.

From the Outside In, on the contrary, objections to various unhealthy aspects of Christianity, some of which are valid, have a certain abstract quality to them because they do not flow from an interior experience of living the Christian life—warts and all. Authentic Christians, on the contrary, are clearly open to listening to the critiques of others and are themselves quite critical at times of aspects of certain beliefs and practices of Christians. The difference between the Outsiders and the Insiders in their critiques is that the latter are able to engage at times in severe criticisms without losing their basic faith commitment because of their overall experience of the richness of the Christian life. As I have mentioned before, as Cardinal Newman expressed it tersely and to the point, "a thousand difficulties do not make a doubt." Christians tend to lose their faith or succumb to existential doubts when they are not living the faith experience at its deepest level. This may not be true in all cases, but overall it seems that it is above all culpable or non-culpable existential ignorance, which explains most departures from the Christian and here specifically the Catholic Christian Church. Certainly it is legitimate and perhaps existentially necessary to engage at times in sharp criticisms, but these always need to be seen within the overall broader Catholic Christian context as a whole. We must also always keep in mind that the Holy Spirit is constantly drawing Christians to ever deeper insights into the implications of their faith that were previously undeveloped and unnoticed. In what follows, we will look at some of the key arguments for saying that certain Christian beliefs and practices are harmful to the health of individuals, societies, and indeed nations in their interactions with one another.

Chapter Thirty-One

The Christian Experience and Its Critics
John Navone

Because human beings have an almost boundless capacity for self-deception, not all persons affirming that they are intelligent, moral or religious are the intelligent, moral or religious persons that they claim to be; nor, by the same token, are all persons who make no claims to being especially intelligent, moral or religious, lacking in these qualities. The Gospel narratives about the clash between Jesus and the religious authorities underscore the dialectical differences in understanding what is genuinely religious and what is a pure sham. Both the religious authorities and Jesus accused one another of being the agents of Satan. In these clashes, Jesus affirmed the only objective basis for making such claims: by their fruits we shall know them. Intelligent, reasonable, and responsible decisions and actions proceed from intelligent, reasonable, and responsible persons. Stupid, unreasonable, and irresponsible decisions and actions proceed from stupid, unreasonable, and irresponsible persons.

In the Judeo-Christian tradition, divine and human love is the distinctive character of an authentically religious life. We are called to love God above all and to love others as ourselves. The Love that calls us into existence is a covenant-creating and covenant-sustaining Love experienced in the communion, community, and communication of the community of faith. The Ten Commandments express the imperative of divine love for an authentically human community, where loving God above all liberates us from the self-idolatry that would reduce the human community to a state of civil war, of *homo homini lupus*. Loving God above all is freedom for loving others as equals.

Jesus, the Incarnate Word of the God who is Love, affirms that "By this shall all know that you are my disciples, if you have love for one another" (Jn 13:35). Mutual love enables knowledge of what is authentically religious. Jesus reveals the befriending God who is known in the community of divine and human friendship: "Greater love has no man than this, that a man lay down his life for his friends" (Jn 15:13); "No longer do I call you servants…but I call you friends" (Jn 15:15).

The divine love that calls the community of faith into existence and sustains its existence can be lost: "Whoever claims to be in light but hates his brother is still in darkness. Anyone who loves his brother remains in light and there is in him nothing to make him fall away" (1 Jn 2:9-10). Although hatred of others renders specious any claim to being religious, self-rightness clearly enables such self-deception. Over the centuries, both the Jewish and Christian communities of faith have had to deal with the problem of their false prophets, the pseudo-religious, whose hatred and falsehood betrayed the true goodness of our loving God. Responsiveness to the love of God grounds the only legitimate claim to being authentically religious. Hearing the Word of God is always a question of living in response to the Word of Love.

Chapter Thirty-Two

Is Self-Reliance Healthier than Believing in God?

Bernard Tyrrell

There is a cluster of objections to the goodness and healthiness of the Christian and specifically Catholic Christian practice of the faith and the existential validity of its beliefs. For example, there is the question of whether the Christian Way makes believers better people than others who lack this faith commitment. Again, there is the objection that religion in general and specifically the Christian religion is a form of child abuse. Similarly, on the national and international front, there is the charge that religious wars are responsible for most of the killing humanity has endured over the centuries. These are the questions—and there are other less crucial ones unanswered here—whose contemporary answers seem to the militant atheists to be highly damaging to religion and which, accordingly, lead a person like Hitchens to declare that "religion poisons everything."

We will first then attempt an answer to the question of whether or not Christian believers are superior in their moral behavior to non-believers? In the ideal order—all other things being equal—it is objectively best to belong explicitly to the Roman Catholic religion in order to best observe the commandments summed up in the love of God and the love of neighbor, as Christ loves the church. But, and here is a major caveat, all other things are often not equal. As T.S. Eliot put it, "between the idea and the reality falls the shadow." Christians generally and more specifically Catholic Christians often do not live up to the practice of the great commandments to which they are called, even though "to whom must is given, much is expected." On the other hand, we have non-Catholic Christians and even secularists who seem to live ordinary and even extraordinary lives of loving others and of following the demands of their conscience. At times, they are willing to give their lives for a truly noble cause.

How is the above possible? Through the invisible mission of the Holy Spirit of Christ from the Father God grants his graces to all human beings of good will who seek to live the best lives they can, even at times heroically, although they do not explicitly understand that it is in Christ and through the Holy Spirit that they live in a lasting fashion a loving life. Indeed, as Karl Rahner observes, a person may be a theist in his head, but a practical atheist in his heart and vice versa a person may be an atheist in his head but a theist in his heart.

The Second Vatican Council and many statements of Blessed John Paul II indicate that the Holy Spirit and the graces dispensed by the Holy Spirit are, in ways that we do not fully understand, at work in all human beings. It is this and this alone, that can explain why non-believers can and often enough do submit to the authentic inspired callings of their conscience to live not only good, but at times saintly lives. It is useful to recall that Jesus told a Roman centurion, who believed that Jesus could heal his servant at a distance, that He had not found so great a faith in all of Israel. Jesus here acknowledged that inspired faith can exist even outside of the hearts of the chosen people. Elsewhere Jesus acknowledged that what seems impossible to men is not impossible to God. Indeed, all things are possible with God.

Chapter Thirty-Two

Is Self-Reliance Healthier than Believing in God?

John Navone

Angry new atheists and agnostics who hate religion do not speak for all atheists and agnostics. Many atheists and agnostics affirm the value of religious faith in God. A Jewish agnostic friend affirms the value of belief in God on the basis of her religious friends who had the courage to face death: "Anything that gives persons the courage to face death is good." Even the religiously indifferent Napoleon promoted religion because it promoted civic friendship, peace, and morality.

The angry new atheists' categorical claims that religion poisons everything is undermined by the common interpretation according to which God's testing Abraham taught, among other things, that the then widespread practice of child-sacrifice was contrary to God's will, and must be put to an end forever.

At the same time, Mr. Hitchens has nothing to say about the historical role of religion, particularly Christianity, in nourishing the soil in which our widely and deeply shared beliefs in liberty, democracy and equality took root and grew strong—a subject dealt with perceptively by Yale professor of computer science David

Gelernter in his recent book *Americanism: The Fourth Great Western Religion*.

Mr. Hitchens' selective outrage over the crimes of allegedly religious individuals and societies contrasts with his apparent obliviousness to the twentieth-century atheist Soviet, Nazi, and Maoist exterminations that surpassed those of all previous centuries combined. Hitchens holds out the naïve utopian hope that eradicating religion will subdue humanity's evil propensities and resolve its enduring questions. He shows no awareness that his atheism, far from resulting from skeptical inquiry, is the rigidly dogmatic premise from which his inquiries proceed, and that it colors all his observations and determines his conclusions.

The Judeo-Christian communities of faith believe that the Origin, Ground, and Destiny of all creation is Goodness Itself; that human beings have the freedom to intelligently and responsibly use or foolishly and irresponsibly abuse the boundless gifts and goods of the Generous One; that we are free to be either humbly grateful or obtusely indifferent to the Generous One. If human freedom is genuine and God really does give us autonomy when we are called into being, and if love is not coercive, we cannot unequivocally assert that everybody is going to behave a certain way. Grace is not a bulldozer that finally makes people do something, whether they are willing or not.

Insofar as we are the created effects of the Creator "effecting" us, we are the objects of God's universal saving love. We are freely responding, positively or negatively, to the grace and call of our Origin, Ground, and Destiny. We do not exist independently of the Ultimate Reality which we inevitably experience as the Question-Raising and Question-Answering Mystery at the heart of our lives, whether or not we have been enlightened by the historical biblical revelation. The quality of that experience is all of a piece with the quality of the conclusion of our life-long experience/process.

The revealed superstructure of human experience illuminates the primordial, preconceptual infrastructure of that experience. John's Gospel tells us that persons recalcitrant to the grace and of call of God within the infrastructure of their experience will be no less recalcitrant at the level of the revealed superstructure: No one recognizes Christ for what He is unless the Father draws him to that re-cognition, that "second knowing" or re-cognition of what one already knows in one's primordial, non-conceptual experience. Christ has given his life/Holy Spirit for all human beings, independently of their knowing about it. That Spirit, we believe, is a "given" for every human life before and after Christ. Our free reaction to the "given" (grace and call of Christ's Holy Spirit) determines whether or not we have accepted it, our new life in the Spirit of the Triune God.

Matthew's Gospel (25) tells of the Son of Man arriving for the judgment, informing people that they had been in touch with him when they had shown compassion for him even without recognizing him. Matthew's text suggests an analogy. Imagine that you have a most enjoyable conversation with a stranger on your way to a lecture/film, only to discover to your astonishment that the individual whose company you had so much enjoyed is the one giving the lecture or the star of the film. Matthew 25 implies that we shall have had experience of the Son of Man long before our realizing it at the final judgment. Matthew 25 assures us of our eventual "So-that-was-You!" knowledge of our historical experience. The experience is primordial and prior to our knowledge of the One experienced! We had met the One in every one that we had experienced.

Chapter Thirty-Three

Breakdown and Redemption

Bernard Tyrrell

One of the charges made against religion is that it is a form of child abuse. The kind of child abuse the atheists are focused on here is that of parents teaching their children specific beliefs and practices of religion from their earliest years. They see this as particularly unhealthy because children are being brainwashed and are becoming poisoned from an early age with destructive beliefs and practices that make it extremely difficult for them to choose true beliefs and ways of behaving that the atheists consider as truly healthy and productive. A first response is that it is actually impossible for parents not to communicate what they believe in and deeply value to their children. There is a symbiosis that occurs whether parents want it to occur or not. Children above all learn from example and so the way the parents live profoundly affects them.

Yet, children as they mature frequently tend to deviate from their parents in the value system they choose to adopt. As one example, Madalyn Murphy O'Hare raised a son as an atheist, but he has become a devout Evangelical. Again, I have been told about a pair of devout Catholic parents who homeschooled their six children as well as allowing them also to attend Catholic schools. The children were extremely talented and all six of them attended

Harvard with scholarships that covered all their college expenses. The end result was that all except their oldest son ended up abandoning their Christian faith.

As a professor at a Catholic University, I have seen similar metamorphoses take place in Catholic children who start out as believers and end up as atheists or at best agnostics. To balance this out, I have seen Catholic children from Catholic schools that end up with a very deep and mature Catholic faith. Overall, I think that the odds favor the latter who attend Catholic instead of secular colleges. At times, I think that Catholics might do well to imitate the Mormon Church, which requires that the young people at a certain age go on missionary journeys proclaiming their faith. This would require that these young people know the basics of their faith before attempting to bring their message to others. This makes a certain sense since Pope Benedict XVI now sees the church as a missionary faith because of the decline of faith in the First World. Perhaps these young Catholics might receive the sacrament of confirmation before going on their missionary journeys.

Today we live in the age of the internet, Facebook, Twitter, and such and one of its unfortunate effects is that there is a great temptation to adopt a relativist view of religion. Pope Benedict XVI has spoken of the "dictatorship of relativism" and not without just cause in the view of this writer. Much of the First World is living in what might be called a "sensate culture." The quest for pleasure, wealth, and power is the great danger of our age. Although what we have written here may cause pessimism about the future, this should not blind us to the incredible richness of the Christian cause, but rather it should stimulate us to delve more deeply into our faith and to recall the words of Jesus: "Have confidence, I have overcome the world." As Navone remarks, "There is far more to life than what the sensate world has to offer."

Chapter Thirty-Three

Breakdown and Redemption

John Navone

Healing, as a part of Christ's ministry, expresses the transforming and enabling power of his grace and of what God does for us. Just as, when we hear of the wisdom of God in the Bible, for example, we think of how God's action make us wise, so when we hear of God's justice we should think of that act by which He makes us just. God's justice, in other words, like his goodness and compassion, is not God's reaction to our behavior, but his initiative, quite irrespective of our behavior. God is free to do what He wills, and his freedom takes the form of acting so as to change us. It is a serious mistake to think that "justification" means a change in God's attitude without effect in us. On the contrary, what changes is that we become the locus of God's free activity. Unprovoked, unconditioned, and unconstrained by any other agent, God steps into the void and chaos of created existence and establishes himself there as God.

The mystery of the cross tells of the place where the wretchedness of the created world and the total failure of human resources or human virtue is most fully exhibited. Where else could we see God's absolute liberty to be God, irrespective of any external conditions? And where but in our own empty and hellish dereliction could we find what it is to trust without reserve in God's freedom exercised for our sake? What gives us ground to stand before God is God: God has in Christ taken his stand in the human world and answered for, taken responsibility for, every human being, quite apart from any achievement or aspiration on the part of humans.

Christian life is essentially the outworking of Christ's life within us, expressing the Spirit of Christ poured into our hearts. The incarnate Lord was not merciful, generous, forgiving, and so on, in order to win approval from heaven, since heaven was his very environment. His good works are the expression of who He is.

The generous self-giving of the Triune God has its imperatives. There is nothing good in us that is not given; therefore, we are, beyond all possibility of repayment, fundamentally indebted. That awareness of indebtedness has the effect of making relative and questionable all our claims as human beings to have an absolute right of disposal over what is concretely and materially ours. We are called to freely give what we have freely received. We have been graced to become gracious towards others. What we believe to be our own is in fact given to us so that it may be shared: it is owed already to those whose need is greater.

What would society look like if a dominant motif in Christian life were gratitude, a detachment from possessions grounded not so much in any doctrine of the evils of the world's goods as in a recognition that God's gifts are restless in the hands of the receiver until they are given again, and that our rights of possession in and over the material world are systematically undermined by the awareness of the givenness of all things, spiritual and material.

The theological principle of God's prior generous action in all things bound up in our relation to him here spills over into some extremely practical considerations. What is it to recognize in the concrete circumstances of one's own prosperity or welfare the presence of divine action? It is, without doubt, to recognize that the apparently static things that secure our prosperity are carriers of God's love, and that therefore they cannot sit still with us; they must not be prevented from being active signs of love. When we try to hold on to them, we make empty our claims to be dependent on God for our spiritual security, because we implicitly deny that God is active in all his gifts. Just as children receive their life from their parents, generous lives reveal the true children of the Generous One.

Chapter Thirty-Four

The Problem of Evil

Bernard Tyrrell

The problem of evil in creation is one of the greatest blocks to accepting the personal God of the monotheistic religions. Antony Flew moved from atheism to deism, but he was not able to take the next crucial step to embrace the God of Love of Christianity because he found the evils in creation so great that he could not reconcile these evils with the existence of a truly loving personal God. Bernard Lonergan at the end of his chapter on religion in his *Method in Theology* also remarks that without faith the world is too evil for a good God to exist. The difference between these two philosophers is similar, but much more dissimilar.

Lonergan in his later period stressed that the philosophy of God should be done within a theological context and his position on the absolutely crucial role of faith in our world explains at least in part his reasons for placing philosophical reflections on God within theology. For Lonergan, we have never existed in a world that was devoid of faith and this makes all the difference. The effects of Christ's saving activity in accord with God's providence were felt immediately after the failure of the first human beings to do God's will as we see even in Genesis and the workings of the Holy Spirit throughout the period of the Jewish Scriptures. This view is confirmed by the Catholic Church in its solemn declaration that the Virgin Mary was preserved from the effects of original sin in the light of the foreseen merits of Jesus Christ. Humanity never existed in a world of pure nature. The gift of a pre-conceptual faith was available to human beings of good will in the instant following the Fall in the theology of Lonergan and Rahner.

But, how then do we explain all the evil in the world even today? The only absolutely radical evil is sin. Lonergan follows Augustine and Aquinas in holding that sin is not an existing being, but rather a privation in the will of what ought to be there but is not. To be precise, for Lonergan, sin is the failure of free will to choose a morally obligatory course of action or its failure to reject a morally obligatory course of action (p. 689 of *Insight*). Sin is irrational and consequently unintelligible. Sin is not an entity or being because it is unintelligible and is not an event, but a failure or absence in the will of a reasonable response to a morally obligatory course of action. It is constituted of what could and ought to be but is not. This is why God is not the cause of sin because it is not an existing being and God only causes what exists. Rather God does not directly or indirectly cause sin, but only permits it. God allows human beings to exercise freedom in their choices, but is not the cause of the privation in the will of the human being of what ought to be there to be there, but is not.

Chapter Thirty-Four

The Problem of Evil

John Navone

Human failure, whether culpable or non-culpable, is a universal human experience. Death, the lot of humankind, is apparently the ultimate failure, raising questions of God's existence, goodness, and an after-life. Whatever the answers, death remains dreadful and communicates a terrible sense of failure.

The failure of history to produce Utopia has disillusioned idealists of every era. Every age records the evil of its failures, its dramas of oppression, collective suffering, deportations, massacres, and humiliations. Every age chronicles fresh social injustices, wars, greed, and exploitation, in which we create tragedy after tragedy for ourselves. The idea that there has to be a human fulfillment *in* history, that the religious, social or political millennium will come in time, rather than at the end of time or outside of time, is debated. Regardless of the position taken in the debate, the fact remains that no age has been without the profound experience of historical failure. The historical process of itself has not produced universal peace and brotherhood. The apocalyptic biblical view of the human condition implies the impossibility of human freedom and fulfillment within the historical process. Disappointment in the outcome of historical events leads to liberation from an illusion or self-deception that temporal beatitude constitutes salvation. Historical failure, whether culpable or not, still remains a kind of dying.

There is also a sense in which the future fails. Frequently persons feel that they have no future, whether in their present historical situation or in terms of an after-life. To be without either kind of future indicates a state of oppression or destitution often reflected in contemporary literature or drama. Having nothing to remember implies having nothing to look forward to; on the other hand, an obsession with evil memories promises a future that is no future at all.

The Christian community of faith's remembrance of the transcending love of its crucified and risen Savior empowers it with a future that transcends the ultimate failure of sin and death; remembering redemption redeems the future, transforming death into a transition in life rather than the ultimate failure of life.

The meaning of things is a part of their reality. The meaning of Jesus' death, Christians believe, is different from any other death. It represents a unique reality, inasmuch as the meaning of a process is only fully understood in the term of that process. The meaning of Jesus' death is only grasped by the resurrection faith in which Jesus' death terminates. Jesus had attached a special meaning to his sufferings and life-giving death, as part of God's plan and purpose (Lk 9:22; 13:32; 18:31-33); they would have important results in which his disciples would share (Lk 22:15-20; 28-30). The disciples believed that this meaning explained their experience of the Crucified and Risen Jesus. Hence, the reality of Jesus' death, as well as that of his suffering and failure that were intimately linked to it, is rooted in the meaning that Jesus had given it and that his disciples recalled. Failure, suffering, and death had been given a new meaning; they had been transformed into a different kind of reality, a new reality, a healing, transforming, and liberating reality.

Through the power and meaning of divine love, everything is a grace working for our good; even failure, suffering, and death are endowed with the possibility of a Theophanous quality that both illuminates and transforms the world. In fact, the wisdom of the cross suggests that perhaps the best way of healing and enlightening the world is through the acceptance of failure, suffering, and death in the name of the absolute truth, love, and goodness of God. These are the effective means of the divine wisdom for the communication of that truth, love, and goodness that save the world by empowering it to transcend those evils that are genuinely lethal to the human spirit. Jesus accepts failure in his Father's name, and his Father accepts the failure of his Son because it is what his Son *is* that counts, rather than how He succeeds by purely human standards. Christians believe that we are ultimately regenerated by this mutual acceptance of Father and Son through the medium of failure and death.

The endurance of suffering, evil, and death is not a passive posture; rather, it requires, in its deepest Christian sense, a radically graced adherence to God, Eternal Life, and Love Itself.

Chapter Thirty-Five

Overcoming Human Failure

Bernard Tyrrell

Besides basic sin, Lonergan speaks of moral evils that result from sin and physical evils in the universe. In our early discussion of original sin we spoke of concupiscence, which is an effect of sin and can lead to sin but is not itself sin. It is a proclivity or weakness that can lead to sin, but it can also be opposed by a good free choice in the face of temptation and result in something good. To experience temptations is not the same thing as to yield to temptations which then involves sin.

Besides basic sin and moral evils there exist physical evils. If God wills the existence of an evolutionary world then physical evils can and do take place, for example, an earthquake occurs in which people are killed. And throughout the long history of the universe there happen false starts, failures to develop properly and so forth. God indirectly wills these physical evils in choosing to create an evolutionary world governed by classical laws, statistical laws, and genetic development. In this kind of universe there are inevitably false starts and incomplete developments.

This leads to the question regarding why bad things happen to good people. At a certain stage of the writings of the Jewish Scriptures the teaching was that good people always prosper and evil people do not. This viewpoint is expressed in the first psalm.

But, later we have the book of Job and the prophecies of Isaiah regarding the righteous individual who suffers. In the teachings of Jesus for the most part there is the message that the righteous can and do suffer. Jesus remarks that God lets the sun shine on the righteous and the unrighteous alike (Mt 5:45). Likewise when the disciples raise questions about a tower that fell and killed people Jesus responds that those who were killed were not necessarily people who were more unrighteous than righteous (Lk 13:4). This is where the "prosperity gospel" fails in its fidelity to the teachings of Jesus. We also often find parables where an example of a righteous person who is suffering is contrasted with an unrighteous person who flourishes. Such is the case in the famed parable of Lazarus and Dives (Lk 16-20). And throughout the Gospels we read again and again about the dangers of riches that are not used properly and how difficult it is for the rich man to get into heaven. To balance this out Jesus himself had rich friends, but they were righteous rather than unrighteous or in need of conversion. And in Matthew 25 we have the famous last judgment scene in which God divides the sheep from the goats. And what is the criterion for this separation? It is based on how people helped or did not help the poor, the hungry, the thirsty, people in prison, and the naked. This parable should force all of us to ask ourselves in what category we think we will find ourselves in the Last Judgment. Jesus taught that it is easy to help out one's own flesh and blood relatives and friends. But, what really counts is how we help the needy of this world. This is what "social justice" is really all about when it is properly understood and practiced.

Atheism Today A Christian Response

Chapter Thirty-Five

Overcoming Human Failure

John Navone

Despite the experience of evil and failure on its many levels, the Christian preserves a fundamental optimism towards the world; not the optimism of agnostic humanism, but of the believer, who knows in faith that the world has been taken radically and irrevocably into the loving care of the Father through and with and in Christ. It is an optimism that endures in and through death, disaster, and sin, because the Christian knows that it is in and through Christ's life-giving death that the power of his resurrection is communicated throughout the world. The Christian must be optimistic, then, but not utopian: optimistic because Christ has been raised from the dead as the first fruits of those who are subjected to God the Father; not utopian, not deluded into thinking that the inherent structures of the world can, of themselves, permanently bring peace and happiness.

Christian realism resists both the tendency to stress this-world values in such a way that the values of the world to come are neglected and the tendency to stress the values of the world to come in such a way that the values of this world are neglected. Either tendency not only excludes true values, but in doing so seriously distorts the values that are retained. Pelagianism, an example of the first distortion, assumes that the human mind and heart can achieve the triumph of the Kingdom of God in this world permanently by mere human means. It often takes the form of some political messianism that stresses the present and disregards the ultimate future. Quietism, the other extreme, is a failure to live up to the Christian vocation to use all the human means that learning and intelligence offer to create good social structures. The Christian seeks to avoid these two extremes of failure, doing everything or doing nothing, by relying on God's grace and contributing to the creation of a new world.

Christian realism recognizes that human failure, which is sin, has penetrated the world so deeply and has so debilitated us that we cannot uphold and practice consistently our highest ideals without the healing of mind and heart, which is the gift of the Holy Spirit. Although a utopian state of dedicated humanism is theoretically possible, there is no historical evidence for its sustained unselfish exercise in human history. Good will, passion, and feverish action do not suffice to preclude future calamities. The assumption that the world must be perfect is often combined with the assumption that all disorder derives from exploitation and sin, so that it becomes a moral and political virtue to hate what is disordered or imperfect since it must be caused by evil, which we must hate in its representatives. Such visions allow no room for human beings in their finiteness, in their history, in their smallness, in their failures.

The Christian vision of failure in the world order and in the individuals who constitute it is that of its Lord who has revealed to us what it means to be moved by the love of God and neighbor. His creative vision accepted the fact of an imperfect, fallible world of limited persons. He has embraced and elevated human finitude: "For it is not as if we had a high priest who was incapable of feeling our weakness with us; but we have one who has been tempted in every way that we are, though he is without sin. Let us be confident, then, in approaching the throne of grace, that we shall have mercy from him and find grace when we are in need of help" (Heb 4:15-16).

The vision of Christ overcomes the human failure to believe that we have nothing beyond ourselves, that our own values are merely what we create for ourselves, that the social complexus of infinite relationships bear the ethical burden as substitute for the person. The vision of Christ comprehends the finitude of the human person and of human society. Christ the compassionate high priest "can sympathize with those who are ignorant or uncertain because he too lives in the limitations of weakness" (Heb 3:2). His vision counters that ideological perfectionist intolerance for allowing mistakes, that modern form of angelism that believes that this world can be paradise. It is embodied in the theological tradition where there is still room for those who hear the Word, but fail to practice it. They are called, especially by themselves, "sinners," and Christians are admonished to love them too somehow. This tradition counters the ideological mood where there no longer seems to be space for failures, where the problems confronting us are believed to be too vast, too pressing, to allow anyone the liberty to fail. It counters the ideologue's self-righteous assumption that "the others" have a monopoly on human failure. Christianity affirms that all of us need our merciful God's redemption because we all fail. It affirms the validity of finite persons who are created by something other than themselves.

Chapter Thirty-Six

Morality and Atheism

Bernard Tyrrell

What is the generative source of morality? Just as Aristotle claimed that all human beings possess a natural desire for knowledge so also all human beings are endowed with a natural desire to be moral. The originating source of the human desire to be authentically moral is innate and a priori. It is the fountainhead of all explicit moral injunctions including the Ten Commandments and other moral demands. It is expressed well by Lonergan in his five transcendental precepts: Be attentive! Be understanding! Be reasonable! Be responsible! Be in love with God and loving!

Morality actively consists in making good value judgments and then actively carrying them out in practice. If we have a natural desire not only for intelligibility and truth, through which we know the existence of things, but also for authentic values and the good why do we often fail to pursue the truly good and worthwhile, but rather opt instead for apparent goods rather than for what is really good? The answer is that we are free to make either authentic or inauthentic choices and to establish a hierarchy of goods or values that is either a morally correct hierarchy of values or a false one. As we have already seen, we are potentially subject to various forms of bias and these biases of either an individual or group nature can skew our process of making correct value judgments and then living in accord with them.

What we are in need of is not only intellectual conversion, but moral and spiritual or religious conversion as well. We have already seen in our chapters on the process of knowing what occurs when we reasonably reach not only an initial understanding of data, but when we rationally weigh the evidence that then leads us to make correct judgments and reach truth and hence reality. Intellectual conversion occurs when we correctly understand and verify the stages of the process by which we reach correct judgments and hence being. Moral conversion consists in developing habits of making good value judgments and acting in accord with them. This is the way that we form our basic character for either good or ill. Character is all important. It means that when we are faced with a choice we spontaneously choose not an apparent good, but what is really good despite the fact that we may suffer in some way as the result of our judgment and action. This is what constitutes a truly good person.

Of course we need the help of divine grace throughout the whole process of forming our character. We do not judge and act authentically unaided by God and the love of God poured into our hearts. But God's grace is always available. Through spiritual or religious conversion, we discern the correct hierarchy of values and habitually act in accord with them. At the very heart of all conversions is God. The atheist claims that we live in an amoral universe since without God we are the sole source of morality and there is then nothing that prevents us from falling prey to relativism and hence setting up our own hierarchy of values, which can be very self-centered. Anything goes. Christianity provides us with the Ten Commandments and the moral teachings of Jesus, which are in best accord with the immanent demand of our conscience, which is to make authentic judgments of fact and value. Above all, Jesus commands us to love not only our family and friends but our enemies as well, to love in fact that way Jesus has modeled for us as the way to form a fully authentic character.

Finally, we should recall from our earlier discussions that God's grace is at work in all human beings of good will and this means that the individual who is an atheist in his or her head, but a theist in the heart will try to mold their character in accord with the most authentic set of moral teachings with which they have contact. There are certain authentic moral teachings in the diverse religions and systems of ethics that exist and here correct discernment will be required. And God's grace will be there aiding authentic character development. Of course everyone falls short and this is where openness to forgiveness is very important. There is no sin that cannot be forgiven except the sin of final and definitive impenitence. Here we must keep in mind that God alone provides us with not only forgiveness for ourselves, but the grace to forgive others regardless of what they have done. God alone sets the basic canon of the authentic hierarchy of values and God alone is the ultimate judge of the human heart. Jesus in the "Our Father" makes it clear that God's forgiveness of our own sins is in accord with the forgiveness we offer to others. He also teaches us that we will be judged by the way we judge others. What is perhaps most important is the exercise of mercy. "Blessed are the merciful for they will receive mercy."

Chapter Thirty-Six

Morality and Atheism

John Navone

The new atheists dismiss the God-of-the-gaps view of a handy God showing up to handle situations beyond our control is inadequate. Kendra Creasy Dean's book *Almost Christian* tells us that this is the view of American teenagers. It lacks Newman's sense of God's presence to our conscience, of God as the Question-Raising-and-Answering Mystery at the heart of our cognitive-affective consciousness, the created effect being affected in every moment of our existence by the uncreated Cause/Spirit effecting it. Their God-of-the-gaps religiosity is a "Teen Spirit" devoid of mysticism, of the intimate loving Presence enabling us to be present to ourselves in the light of its loving and enlightening presence. Their friendly Handyman God is no substitute for the Happiness Itself (*Ipsa Felicitas*) of Aquinas or "Jesus, Joy of Man's Desiring" of Bach, our Alter Ego/ Friend. The "Teen Spirit" is deaf to the Jesus of John's Gospel calling us "friends." They are clueless about Jesus: they have eyes that do not see this Jesus and ears that do not hear him. They are devoid of what Rahner would call the "mystical experience of Jesus," and of what Friedrich Heiler notes as the basic aspects of religious experience in the major world religions: the experience of a transcendent reality, immanent in our hearts, that is supreme beauty, truth, righteousness, goodness; that is love, mercy and compassion, approached in repentance, self-denial and prayer; encountered in love of our neighbor, even of our enemies; that love of God is the way to God, so that happiness is conceived as the intimate knowledge and communion with God.

Recent studies suggest that religious people tend to be happier and more fulfilled in their lives than non-believers. Martin Seligman, the psychologist who has put positive psychology, the discipline known as the science of happiness, on the map, argues that lasting levels of happiness can be influenced by changing your life. "Becoming religious" is in his top five things to do. These results are echoed by the economist, Professor Richard Layard, who in his 2005 book, *Happiness: lessons from new science*, presented evidence that having no faith had a more detrimental impact on happiness than losing a job. All in all the evidence suggests that practices of faith tend to have positive effects on people's lives. The impact of faith assessed across a number of metrics, shows, for example, the likelihood that an individual will drink excessively or take up drugs decreases significantly if they go to church, temple, or mosque. Actively religious persons are less likely to commit crime, get divorced, commit suicide, or suffer from depression.

Just why is it that religion has positive effects? A first possibility assigns efficacy to the proscriptive character of religion. World faiths carry moral weight: they encourage, if not insist, that their faithful adherents do not do things like take drugs, commit crimes, or practice infidelity. There are other possibilities. Richard Layard has suggested that the issue is emotional habits. He argues that religious practices train individuals to control their feelings. In his book on happiness, Layard discussed *The Spiritual Exercises* of Ignatius of Loyola, noting how the saint sought to nurture several attitudes that modern science has demonstrated are essential for well-being. Ignatius encouraged his readers to praise God, that is, to learn to be grateful. He urged them to serve God, which had the effect of dissolving egotism by drawing attention away from yourself. He encouraged a spirit of detachment/indifference that built up resilience in the face of life's difficulties.

Mark Vernon, author of *The Big Questions: God* (Quercus, 2012) affirms that religions are good at building community and nurturing kindness because they open up adherents to that source of life, or spiritual sustenance, that is expansive of our humanity. They offer practices that, over time, transform the soul. It is variously called salvation, eternal life, or enlightenment. Goodwill and well-being may follow; also, they may not. But when they do, Vernon believes that they are happy by-products of the main task, which is not actually to have a successful life. It is, rather, to come to know God, to become the friend of God. To whom are you expressing gratitude for life if not God? The blind mechanisms of evolution? Or, it might be noted that you do not become religious in order to be happy; and if you tried to do so the strategy would fail you.

Gone are the days when faith could be simply written off. A basic and obvious question is being avoided by atheistic writers: Might human well-being actually have something to do with God?

Human beings have both wonderful capacities and severe limits. We seek truth, goodness, and beauty, despite the inevitability of death. We wrestle with answers to the big questions: What should I live for and why? What should I believe, and why should I believe it? What is morality, and where does it come from? What kind of a person should I be? What is the meaning of life, and what should I do in order to lead a fulfilling life? We are meaning-making and significance-seeking animals, yet we have difficulty creating satisfying meanings solely from within the horizons of the immanent world we occupy. In any case, religion has been the primary way that human cultures have answered these life questions.

Chapter Thirty-Seven

Death: The Final End or Prelude to the Resurrection?

Bernard Tyrrell

C ontemporary atheists believe that no one remains alive after death. Most contemporary Christians believe that all human beings eventually will be raised from the dead either with glorified bodies or in a negative state that the damned undergo in their bodies and finally in a transformed cosmos. Paul in Romans 8 suggests that the whole of creation is groaning in travail until the final resurrection takes place. The glorification of the cosmos does not imply the complete destruction of the present universe, but its transformation. If God creates everything from nothing and continuously holds it in existence then God is perfectly capable of effecting not the destruction, but rather a glorious transformation of the cosmos. Theological reflection also leads us to conclude that even the pains suffered by non-human life forms somehow will be transformed into a happy state in which the lamb will exist in a peaceful relationship with the lion and so likewise with all other non-human creatures.

Someone might object that we have omitted from our belief in an afterlife the belief in karma—good and bad—which accrues to an individual in their lifetime and the belief in ongoing reincarnations that millions upon millions adhere to with conviction. Only when an individual is totally enlightened will this individual finally be liberated from this process of reincarnation. One reason for objecting to this view is that in this belief system you are born as a blessed person or a cursed person resulting from the karma of your previous reincarnation. This means that you deserved whatever situation you are born into and the result of this is that you are judged as either bad or good depending on the circumstances into which you are born. This goes against the belief that we are all born as equal before God and that you must not be judged as good or bad in the light of the circumstances of your birth. Such a belief system operates at least implicitly with less of an impetus toward social justice than do some Western monotheistic belief systems. Another reason for objecting to this belief system is that few if any people recall what or who they previously were and hence have no memory of how precisely to deal with their present situation in the light of their past mistakes. These reasons among many others are what lead us to the rejection of this type of belief system about an afterlife.

Catholics believe that each human being has an immortal soul that survives death. Likewise they believe that there is a particular judgment and a general judgment. The first takes place immediately after death and it decides the eternal destiny of the person: heaven, purgatory for a time, or hell. The individual soul immediately is placed in one of these three states. Aquinas says that it is not natural for the soul to be separated from the body and that it maintains a relation to matter but that this will be fully rectified in the general resurrection in which God judges all, restores the unity of the body-soul relationship of the individual and effects the resurrection of all and the glorification of the universe. Karl Rahner speculates that upon death the individual undergoes a particular resurrection as did Jesus and Mary. Mary as the perfect discipline in her assumption of body and soul into heaven prefigures the particular resurrection of each individual upon dying. However, what remains of singular importance is the resurrection either at death or at the end of the world in a state of glorious transformation.

How important for Christians is it to believe in a resurrection? It is all important! Paul makes it abundantly clear that if Jesus Christ was not personally raised up from the dead then we are still in our sins. In fact, he says that if we are not to be raised from the dead then our living the Christian way of life is without meaning and that we among all peoples are the most to be pitied. It is not enough to say that, although Jesus Christ was not raised from the dead, nonetheless "the cause of Jesus lives on." The "cause" of Jesus is then at most a set of moral teachings akin to those of Confucius or the many other teachers of morals. The heart of Christianity is the death and resurrection of Jesus Christ and if that belief is omitted Christianity falls apart.

Chapter Thirty-Seven

Death: The Final End or Prelude to the Resurrection?

John Navone

Assuring us that we are advancing toward a world that will be made perfect by technology and science, the new atheists blame religion for genocide, injustice, persecution, backwardness, and intellectual and sexual repression. Theirs is both the illusion that, under the guise of science or rationalism, we can free ourselves from the limitations of human nature and perfect the human species, and that we are morally advancing as a species, despite the fact that little scientific or historical evidence supports this idea. Individuals and societies are subject to both moral and cultural progress and decline. Our personal and collective histories alternate between periods of light and periods of darkness. Individuals and societies not only develop, but also suffer break downs. We may advance materially without advancing morally. The belief in an ineluctable collective moral progress ignores the inherent fallibility of human nature as well as the tragic reality of human history. The illusion that we can master our destiny, while ignoring the truth of our human condition, has serious consequences.

Without an ethic based on the truth of things, one that takes into account the limits and precariousness of the human situation, we cannot realistically begin to cope with our individual, social and political problems. Our utopian schemes generally finish miserably.

The obscurantist new atheists dismiss the religious impulse that addresses something just as real and concrete as the pursuit of scientific knowledge: the human hunger for the sacred, the transcendent, the *mysterium tremendum et fascinans*. God is, as Aquinas argues, the power that allows us to be ourselves. God is the call to marvel, wonder, and reverence. We are ingrained with this impulse which asks: What are we? Why are we here? What, if anything, are we supposed to do? What does it all mean? Science, while illuminating these questions, cannot answer them. Scientific laws cannot replace moral laws.

Our openness to the transcendent inspires us to create myths and stories to explain who we are, where we came from, and our place in the cosmos. Myth is more than a primitive scientific theory that can be discarded in an industrialized age. We all stoke the fires of symbolic mythic narratives to give meaning, coherence, and purpose to our lives. The language of science is now used by many atheists to express the ancient longings for human perfectibility. According to them, science, rather than religion, is the way from paradise lost to paradise regained. The rationalists of the Enlightenment taught that the godless religion of scientific method could be applied to all aspects of human life, an application that would lead to a better world. They saw that the universe as ruled exclusively by consistent laws which could be explained mathematically or scientifically. Knowledge of these laws sufficed for understanding ourselves and our universe. The disparity between the rational person and the instinctive, irrational person would be solved through the education and scientific knowledge that would eradicate superstition and ignorance. Those who could not be educated and reformed, radical Enlightenment thinkers began to argue, should be eliminated so they could no long poison society. The Jacobins were among the first of the totalitarians who justified murder by invoking supposedly enlightened ideals (Chris Hedges, *I Don't Believe in Atheists: The Dangerous Rise of the Secular Fundamentalist*, London: Continuum, 2008, p. 18) Their radical experiment in human engineering was embodied in the Republic of Virtue and The Reign of Terror, which saw thousands executed. Belief in the moral superiority of Western civilization allowed colonial powers to exterminate people of "inferior races."

The delusional dream of human perfectibility or salvation though science clashes with the religious realism of the community, whose faith is grounded in an authentically religious conversion, responding to the grace and call of the transcendent Good, True, and Beautiful for our ultimate happiness and fulfillment. Such personal transformation unfetters the mind and heart from prejudices that blunt reflection and self-criticism. If self-knowledge of individuals and societies is the beginning of wisdom, to know ourselves is to accept our limitations and imperfections.

Chapter Thirty-Eight

Faith, Belief, Reason, and Resurrection
Bernard Tyrrell

Sam Harris entitles his best seller *The End of Faith*. "End" is a word that expresses goal and purpose as well as termination or fading into obsolescence as Harris intends the word. For Christians the goal of faith is the realization of the reality of the resurrection and the face to face vision of God. There are cradle Christians and individuals who convert to Christianity at a later time. Both groups of Christians at some time in their lives are challenged to provide reasons for the faith that is in them and for the resurrection. For Christians or at least for Catholic Christians reason and revelation cannot be opposed to one another since they are both gifts of the same God.

As we have seen the inner light of faith is what empowers one to believe in the Judeo-Christian revelation. For a grown person who converts to Christianity and specifically Catholic Christianity there comes a point when they reach the rational conclusion that it is intelligent, reasonable, and responsible to convert to Christian beliefs. But, it requires the infusion of the interior light of faith for a person to see that it is not only makes sense to do so rationally and responsibly, but also that it is indeed inwardly compelling for one freely to do so. This is because no one can give their assent to believe in Jesus Christ unless the grace of the Father draws them to do so. However, for those of good will who have no knowledge of the Gospel of Jesus Christ God does pour forth the gift of God's own love, of which faith is the eye, into their hearts but their belief in Jesus Christ is implicit rather than explicit. Karl Rahner thus speaks of the "anonymous Christian" and Lonergan accepts the validity of this reality without using Rahner's terminology.

As one regards the central truth of Christianity that Jesus Christ died for us and rose from the dead, one can very fruitfully employ reason to show from analysis of the biblical texts and the earliest Christian traditions that there seems to be no other reasonable alternative to belief in the resurrection. Yet, one cannot demonstrate conclusively with reason alone that Jesus rose from the dead. Still, analysis of the available evidence shows it as uniquely probable. Here we move beyond reason to faith and belief. Perhaps the best book available on the resurrection of Jesus from the dead is N.T. Wright's *The Resurrection of the Son of God*. It provides a very strong challenge to those who deny belief in the resurrection and it is to be highly recommended.

Contemporary atheists who deny the resurrection show that their knowledge of biblical and theological works such as that of N.T. Wright and other outstanding religious scholars is woefully lacking. And what is freely asserted is also freely denied. Never before in our history has there been a more abundant richness of techniques and methods for studying the Scriptures as to their antiquity and unique character than we have today. Thus, far from eliminating basic Christian beliefs from serious consideration, never have we had more evidential proofs for the validity of Christian claims than we have today.

Chapter Thirty-Eight

Faith, Belief, Reason, and Resurrection

John Navone

The Christian Scriptures never presents the resurrection of Jesus as a resuscitation or a return to his former mode of terrestrial existence, like that of Lazarus (Jn 11:43-44; 12:1-2). Jesus is never portrayed as inhabiting the earth for forty days or appearing as someone who had been ensconced behind a curtain. Indeed Luke (24: 37-39) strives explicitly to reject the idea that He was like a spook.

Though the Christian Scriptures does not say so explicitly, it implies repeatedly that when the risen Christ appeared, He appeared from the glorious presence of his Father: "Christ was raised from the dead by the glory of the Father" (Rom 6:4). And the risen Christ asks his disciples on the road to Emmaus, "Did not the Christ have to suffer these things and enter into his glory?" (Lk 24:26). Moreover, the only difference between the appearance of the risen Christ to Paul on the road to Damascus and that to the others earlier was, in reality, a temporal one: it happened to Paul after Pentecost. This has to be recognized despite the Lucan differences of descriptive details.

Whereas the risen Christ who appears to his disciples insists on his identity, he is also said to have appeared "in another form"

(Mk 16:12). He was first recognized by neither Cleophas and his companion (Lk 24:16) nor Mary Magdalene (Jn 20:14-16). However one might explain this, one must recall the connection of Paul's admission that there is a difference between a "physical body" sown in death and a "spiritual body" raised from death (1 Cor 15:42-44). When Paul tries to describe the risen body, he identifies it expressly with what is not "body," that is, "spirit." This is not a rhetorical oxymoron; rather Paul tells us how we should envision the risen Christ and his glorified body.

They kerygma/proclamation of early Christianity did not content itself to affirm merely that Jesus was alive or that He was a living influence in the lives of his followers. It included the affirmation that Jesus had been "raised" to a state of glory in the presence of the Father, and that would have had to mean "bodily." The bodily resurrection of Jesus to glory is at the heart of Christian faith and proclamation.

Christian Scriptures passages dealing with the "ascension" of Jesus attempt to describe the complex phase of his existence that we variously refer to as his resurrection, exaltation, ascension, or transit to the Father, along with his continued presence to his community of faith in his life-giving Spirit. This complex is, in the proper sense, the "paschal mystery." The Risen Christ's presence among his followers is through the Spirit, the "promise of my Father" (Lk 24:49; Acts 1:4). He would also be present to them "in the breaking of the bread" as the Emmaus incident implies (Lk 24:35).

About the Authors

Bernard Tyrrell, S.J. is emeritus professor of Religious Studies and Philosophy at Gonzaga University. He completed his doctoral studies at Fordhan University and enjoys a doctorate in philosophy and an M.A. in Philosophy at Gonzaga University, and an M.A. in Theology at Santa Clara University. He has taught at the Jesuit School of Theology at Berkeley, the Jesuit School of Theology of Toronto, Canada, the University of San Francisco, and a variety of other universities and institutes. Among his books are *Bernard Lonergan's Philosophy of God, Christotherapy I, Christotherapy II, Christointegration* and many articles and reviews. His Christotherapy books are still in print and the first Christotherapy book has been translated into many languages. He is most known for his many works on Lonergan and for his expertise in philosophy, theology, and psychology.

John Navone, S.J. is a Seattle-born emeritus professor of Theology of the Pontifical Gregorian University, where he completed his doctoral studies and taught from 1967 to 2007. During this period, he taught summer schools at both Seattle University and Gonzaga University in Spokane. His doctoral dissertation, *History and Faith in the Thought of Alan Richardson* (1966) was the first book by a Catholic published by the SCM Press in London. He has written extensively on narrative theology and the theology and spirituality of beauty: *Everyman's Odyssey* (1974), *Tellers of the Word* (1981), *Gospel Love: A Narrative Theology, Seeking God in Story* (1990), *Towards a Theology of Beauty* (1996), *Enjoying God's Beauty* (1999). He has also written books on Biblical theology: *Themes of St. Luke* (1970), *Lead Radiant Spirit – Our Gospel Quest* (2001). He won the National Italian Capri-S. Michele prize for his book, *The Land and the Spirit of Italy* (1998), published in Italian and English. He is also a regular contributor to *Theology* (London), *Parabola* (New York), *The Journal of Dharma* (India), *La Civilita Cattolica* (Rome), *New Blackfriars* (Oxford), *Milltown Studies* and *Studies* (Dublin), The Irish *Theological Quarterly* and *Philosophical Studies* (Maynooth, Ireland).